OVID'S
ART OF IMITATION

MNEMOSYNE

BIBLIOTHECA CLASSICA BATAVA

COLLEGERUNT

W. DEN BOER • W. J. VERDENIUS • R. E. H. WESTENDORP BOERMA

BIBLIOTHECAE FASCICULOS EDENDOS CURAVIT

W. J. VERDENIUS, HOMERUSLAAN 53, ZEIST

SUPPLEMENTUM QUADRAGESIMUM SEPTIMUM

KATHLEEN MORGAN

OVID'S
ART OF IMITATION

PROPERTIUS IN THE AMORES

LUGDUNI BATAVORUM E. J. BRILL MCMLXXVII

OVID'S ART OF IMITATION

PROPERTIUS IN THE AMORES

BY

KATHLEEN MORGAN

LUGDUNI BATAVORUM E. J. BRILL MCMLXXVII

ISBN 90 04 04858 8

CONTENTS

CHAPTER ONE

INTRODUCTION

Ovid's frequent use of imitation in all of his extant works has long been recognized. As early as the mid-nineteenth century the compilation of a comprehensive list of Ovid's imitations was attracting the attention of scholars. Reminiscences of Catullus, Tibullus, Propertius, Ennius, Lucretius, Vergil and Horace, wherever they appeared in the Ovidian corpus, were catalogued by Anton Zingerle. [1] Later work on the problem generally followed Zingerle's lead, i.e. the identification of lines and passages as imitations was paramount. Analysis and interpretation of how and why Ovid imitated as he did was generally secondary. [2]

If, however, we narrow the scope of the problem by considering only Ovid's imitations in the *Amores*, the situation changes. The *Amores* were written by Ovid in his youth and developed out of the already well-defined Roman elegiac tradition. Gallus, Tibullus and Propertius had already gone before, Ovid himself tells us. [3] Perhaps these facts—Ovid's admission of his debt to his predecessors and his youth when he composed the first edition of the *Amores*—have led to the more thorough examination of imitation in the *Amores*.

One need only look to various editions of Propertius and Ovid's *Amores* to see evidence of this scholarly interest. The most complete lists of Propertian reminiscences in Ovid's elegy are offered by Munari in his edition of the *Amores* and by Schuster and Dornseiff

---

[1] A. Zingerle, *Ovidius und sein Verhältnis zu den Vorgängern und gleichzeitigen Römischen Dichtern*. 3 Hefte. (Innsbruck, 1869-71.) In this study unless stated otherwise the quotations of Propertius are from E. A. Barber, *Sexti Properti Carmina*[2] (Oxford, 1960); those of the *Amores* are from E. J. Kenney, *P. Ovidi Nasonis Amores, Medicamina Faciei Femineae, Ars Amatoria, Remedia Amoris* (Oxford, 1961).

[2] Another early list was compiled by C. Ganzenmüller, "Aus Ovids Werkstatt" *Philologus* 70 (1911) 274-311. Interest in Ovidian studies resumed in the late fifties. The following articles include some attempt at analysis of imitation: J. A. Richmond, "On Imitation in Ovid's 'Ibis' and in the 'Halieutica' Ascribed to Him," in *Atti del Convegno Internazionale Ovidiano*, Vol. II (Rome, 1959) 9-57; F. Bömer, "Ovid und die Sprache Vergils", *Gymnasium* 66 (1959) 268-88; J. Ferguson, "Catullus and Ovid" *AJP* 81 (1960) 337-57.

[3] *Tr.* 4.10.53-4.

in the Teubner Propertius. [4] Other editors mention specific imitations, often with brief comments, in their notes. [5] The most comprehensive study, however, is that of Rudolf Neumann published in 1919. [6] Neumann's work attempts to go beyond the earlier efforts of Zingerle and Ganzenmüller, who were primarily compiling lists of imitations. His goals, as he himself stated them, were to discover what themes (*argumenta*) Ovid took from Propertius, to show how Ovid turned these themes to his own use, to ascertain how much of the *Amores* was Ovid's independent creation (*ex Ovidi ingenio nata*) and why Ovid wanted to imitate Propertius. [7]

Neumann's work is invaluable in many ways. His judgment on which lines of the *Amores* are Propertian imitations provides at least a starting point for scholars interested in the problem. He has tried to facilitate analysis by grouping the Propertian echoes according to type: single words, short thoughts, basic themes, and entire poems. [8] He recognizes Ovid's tendency to rewrite Propertius in a lighter, more jocular way. [9] He gives Ovid credit for putting his own stamp on any borrowed material. [10] Yet in many ways, Neumann is inadequate. He never defines his criteria for recognizing Propertian imitations, and indeed, often talks of themes which are only vaguely similar. He sees imitation in every similarity of thought, never taking into account the traditions of the genre in general. Just because both Propertius and Ovid wrote poems about dyeing the hair, does not, as Neumann claims, mean that Ovid was directly copying Propertius. [11] Or when Ovid says, *ingenio causas*

---

[4] F. Munari, *P. Ovidi Nasonis Amores*[5] (Firenze, 1970); M. Schuster and F. Dornseiff, *Sex. Propertii Elegiarum Libri IV*[2] (Leipzig, 1958).

[5] Among these are M. Rothstein, *Die Elegien des Sextus Propertius*[2], 1st and 2nd parts (Berlin, 1920, 1924); H. E. Butler and E. A. Barber, *The Elegies of Propertius* (Oxford, 1933); P. J. Enk, *Sex. Propertii Elegiarum Libri Primus (Monobiblos), Secundus*, 1st and 2nd parts (Leiden, 1946, 1962); P. Brandt, *P. Ovidi Nasonis Amorum Libri Tres*[2] (Hildesheim, 1963; repr. of 1911 ed.); J. A. Barsby, *Ovid's Amores, Book One* (Oxford, 1973).

[6] R. Neumann, *Qua ratione Ovidius in Amoribus scribendis Properti elegiis usus sit* (Diss. Göttingen, 1919). Hereafter cited Neumann.

[7] Neumann (*supra*, note 6), 7.

[8] *Ibid.*

[9] Neumann, 124. This "new" tone, so different from the tone of earlier Latin love elegy, was not generally acknowledged by scholars until after E. Reitzenstein, "Das neue Kunstwollen in den *Amores* Ovids" *RhM* 84 (1935) 62-88.

[10] Neumann, 125.

[11] Neumann, 42-44.

tu dabis una meo (*Am.* 2.17.34), should we really believe that he is specifically echoing Prop. 2.1.4 or 2.30.40? [12] It seems more likely that Ovid is repeating a cliché of the genre.

Because Neumann is willing to judge Ovid's work as imitation on the basis of similarity of subject matter alone, he comes to the conclusion that almost the entire *Amores* is dependent upon Propertius. There are, of course, important and indeed lengthy imitations of Propertius within the *Amores*, but Neumann's position gives Ovid too little credit for being a poet in his own right. [13] In addition, Neumann too often states that Ovid has borrowed a Propertian line or turned a Propertian idea to his own use without any attempt to show why Ovid used the particular Propertian passage where he did. [14] His statement of purpose notwithstanding, Neumann's study concentrates on where and how much Ovid borrowed from Propertius with very little emphasis on why he imitated what he did.

Neumann's view of Ovid as over-dependent on Propertius developed out of a very broad definition of what constitutes imitation. In this study imitations shall be determined on the basis of something more concrete than Neumann's *sententiae* and *argumenta*. Only by establishing philological criteria for imitation can the pitfalls created by the thematic traditions of the genre be avoided. These criteria include similarity in choice of words, position of the words in the line, metrical anomalies, structural development of a particular passage, and other concrete evidence which can be linked to the work of an earlier author. Once imitation has been established by this method, similarities of theme or thought may become important, but the philological evidence for imitation must exist independently of the thematic parallels. The danger of error will

---

[12] Neumann, 16.

[13] I. M. Le M. Du Quesnay, "The *Amores*" in J. W. Binns (ed.), *Ovid* (London, 1973) 1-48 has taken up Neumann's position. "Perhaps the most significant aspect of the *Amores* when viewed as a single collection is Ovid's obvious desire to recall to the reader the first three books of Propertius. Every poem in the collection contains echoes of Propertian imagery and phraseology: many of the poems clearly have a single model in Propertius; others are expansions and variations of themes which form only part of a single poem in his predecessor." (6).

[14] For example, Neumann's conclusions about *Am.* 1.8, which he has clearly shown to be a direct imitation of Prop. 4.5, are simply: "Ovidium . . . duo exemplaria respexisse vidimus, comoediam novam et imprimis Properti elegiam IV. 5. Simul praecepta rhetorica secutus est." (122).

still exist, of course, since any list of imitations must ultimately be somewhat subjective. Still, it is fairer to Ovid to demand strict proof of imitation rather than to assume, with Neumann, that the slightest similarity of thought indicates Propertian influence. If there are fewer imitations, they also gain importance within the context of the individual poems. We can consider them as occasional decorations instead of the basic material from which Ovid fashioned the *Amores*.

Adherence to philological criteria for determining imitation should also help overcome the problems raised by possible influences on both Ovid and Propertius by authors now lost to us. The most important of these is Gallus, whom Ovid names in *Tr.* 4.10 as the first of his elegiac predecessors. Although various attempts have been made to determine his influence on his successors, in general this early elegist remains a mystery. [15] Yet even if Gallus strongly influenced both Propertius and Ovid by establishing various types of poems or themes as the common material of the genre, even if they both imitated him at times, it seems unlikely that we could mistake Gallus' influence for Propertius', if we adhere to the philological method described above. For that to happen, both Ovid and Propertius would have had to imitate the same lines of Gallus with tremendous precision. The possibility exists but only remotely. Confusion which might result from the influences of other genres, such as New Comedy, will be minimal for the same reason. [16]

---

[15] A good general description of Gallus and his probable role in creating Roman elegy can be found in F. Jacoby, "Zur Entstehung der römischen Elegie" *RhM* 60 (1905) 67-81. Gallus' possible influence on Propertius is discussed by H. Tränkle, *Die Sprachkunst des Properz und die Tradition des lateinischen Dichtersprache, Hermes* Einzelschr. 15 (1960) 22-25. L. Winniczyk, "Cornelius Gallus und Ovid" *Deutsche Akademie der Wissenschaften, Berlin. Sektion für Altertumswissenschaft* 22 (1960) 24-36, tries to point to specific lines in the *Amores* which Gallus influenced, but her arguments are unconvincing. The most comprehensive treatment of Gallus is the recent book by D. O. Ross, Jr., *Backgrounds to Augustan Poetry: Gallus, Elegy and Rome* (Cambridge, 1975).

[16] Thematic parallels between New Comedy and Latin elegy have long been recognized. For a summary of previous work, see A. Day, *The Origins of Latin Love-Elegy* (Oxford, 1938) 85-101, or J. C. Yardley, "Comic Influences in Propertius," *Phoenix* 26 (1972) 134-139. F. Leo, *Plautinische Forschungen*[2] (Berlin, 1912) 140-57, felt that these parallels could only be explained by postulating the existence of Hellenistic love elegy. For refutations of Leo, see Jacoby (*supra*, note 15) 42; Day, 1-36; G. Luck, *The Latin Love Elegy* (New York, 1960) 34-38. The existence of a personal erotic tradition in Hellenistic elegy is no longer generally accepted.

The chronology and dating of the *Amores* and the elegies of Propertius is a problem much less easily dismissed. The generally accepted dates for the publication of Prop. I-III are 28-22 B.C. [17] The first edition of the *Amores*, which consisted of five books rather than three, was probably completed around 15 B.C. [18] We can thus assume that Ovid was familiar even in his first edition with Prop. I-III. It is very difficult, however, to date Propertius' fourth book. A reference at 4.11.66 indicates that that poem was written after 16 B.C., but beyond that there are no clues. Propertius was dead by 2 A.D.,[19] so Book IV could have appeared any time between 15 B.C. and 2 A.D. The earliest possible date would mean that Ovid had access to it for both his first and second editions of the *Amores*. Any date after 15 B.C. would mean that Ovid imitated from Prop. IV only in poems he revised or wrote for the second edition of the *Amores*. The exact date of the second edition is disputed, but it was sometime around 1 A.D. [20] The situation is further complicated by the fact that Ovid often heard Propertius recite his poems. [21] He thus had access to unpublished material. While the problem of the exact dates and relationship of Prop. IV to the *Amores* may ultimately be insoluable, a careful

---

[17] Butler and Barber (*supra*, note 5) xxii-xxiii; P. J. Enk (*supra*, note 5: *Liber Primus*, part 1) 16-19; L. A. MacKay, "Umbrian Rimbaud" *G&R* 17 (1970) 177-83, would prefer 26-22 B.C., but his argument centers around a birthdate for Propertius of 41 B.C. G. Williams, *Tradition and Originality in Roman Poetry* (Oxford, 1968) 480-95, claims Propertius published all three books at once but he does not dispute the 22 B.C. *terminus post quem*.

[18] For early bibliography on the dating of the *Amores*, see E. Martini, *Einleitung zu Ovid, Schriften der philosophischen Fakultät der deutschen Universität in Prag*, 12 Band (1933), 27. F. Munari (*supra*, note 4) xiv, says that 15 B.C. is "l'opinione generalmente accettata." A. Cameron, "The First Edition of Ovid's *Amores*" *CQ* 18 (1968) 320-33, agrees with the 15 B.C. *terminus post quem*. However, R. P. Oliver, "The First Edition of the *Amores*" *TAPA* 76 (1945) 191-215, would have the first edition published around 20 B.C.

[19] *R.A.* 763-4:

carmina quis potuit tuto legisse Tibulli
   vel tua, cuius opus Cynthia sola fuit ?

[20] A. Cameron (*supra*, note 18) claims it was published two years before the *Ars*, whose composition can be dated to after 1 B.C. (*Ars* 1.179). Others, on the basis of *Am.* 2.18.19, would have *Amores*² published after the *Ars*. These include Kraus, "Ovidius Naso" *RE* 18¹ (1942), 1921; Marg, review of H. Frankel, *Ovid, Gnomon* 21 (1949) 50.

[21] *Tr.* 4.10.45-6.

study of Ovid's imitations of Prop. IV will shed some additional light on the matter.

Detecting the Propertian imitations in the *Amores* by whatever method can only be the first step in a modern study of Ovidian imitation. Almost as important is the discovery of the methods and motives which governed Ovid's selection of Propertian material and his incorporation of it into his own elegy. Ovid's reputation has always been that of the mere versifier, a reputation which perhaps can be traced back to the words of the poet himself. [22] In antiquity, his *ingenium*, not his *ars*, was stressed, [23] and indeed the metrical polish of his verse, combined with its prolific quantity and the general lightness of his tone, is still influencing modern Ovidian scholarship. [24] Yet a gift for writing fluent and polished verse does not necessarily exclude one from the ranks of the serious artist and the careful poet.

This study proposes not only to establish clearly Propertian imitations in the *Amores*, but also to illuminate Ovid's artistry. By studying his use of imitation, we shall see how carefully Ovid planned his poems in order to achieve his desired effects. No matter how light his tone, no matter how fluent his distichs, Ovid was above all an artist capable of achieving rich and subtle nuances. [25] Imitation of his predecessors was one means to this end.

---

[22] *Tr.* 4.10.25-6:

> sponte sua carmen numeros veniebat ad aptos,
>   et quod temptabam scribere versus erat.

[23] Quint. *Inst.* x.1.88; x.1.98; Seneca, *N.Q.* III.27.13.

[24] For example, G. P. Goold, "Amatoria Critica" *HSCP* 69 (1965) 1-107: ". . . the poet (Ovid) has instinctively evolved a large repertoire of formulaic epithets and tags, together with numerous devices to admit them, which enable him to versify rapidly. This naturally leads to a high degree of metrical virtuosity, but a corresponding absence of profundity. . ." (24). Or T. W. Dickson, "Borrowed Themes in Ovid's *Amores*" *CJ* 59 (1964) 175-80: "It seems fair to regard the *Amores* as sportive exercises in versifying by which Ovid was training himself for more serious poetry. . ." (180).

[25] For an example of an extremely subtle effect, see J. A. Barsby, "*Desultor amoris* in *Amores* 1.3" *CP* 70 (1975) 44-45. Barsby links the word *desultor* to the historical figure Dellius, to whom Horace's *Carm.* 2.3 is addressed. He then makes a case for an echo of 2.3 in *Am.* 1.3.17-18. That Ovid was capable of such subtlety in his allusions will be demonstrated below.

CHAPTER TWO

THE PROGRAMMATIC POEMS

It is to be expected that Ovid would be influenced by his elegiac predecessors in his composition of the programmatic poems of the *Amores*. Any Augustan poet dedicated to the slender Muse of love elegy faced a difficult problem. On the one hand, there were strong pressures favoring the production of serious, socially significant poetry. Both the Roman ethos and the programs of Augustus tended to move the poet towards becoming a *vates* in the Vergilian meaning of the term.[1] On the other hand, the influence of Callimachus and the Alexandrian movement directed these same poets to favor the graceful and light over the heavy and pompous.[2] Different poets solved the conflict in different ways. Vergil progressed from bucolics to Roman epic, thus fulfilling the *vates* role. Horace and Propertius both lingered much longer over their personal, lighter poetry, and both wrote numerous poems defending the decision not to write in a more serious and public-spirited way.[3]

Propertius' poems of explanation are ultimately derived from his mentor, Callimachus. The *recusatio* poem can be traced back to the *Aetia* preface 19-20, where Callimachus calls epic a μέγα ψοφέουσαν ἀοιδήν, and refuses to write it.[4] This basic idea is then developed by the Roman poets into a derogatory statement about

---

[1] See J. K. Newman, *The Concept of Vates in Augustan Poetry*, Collection Latomus 89 (Brussels, 1967).

[2] For a good description of the true meaning of the Callimachean revolution (not simply long poems *vs.* short ones), see J. K. Newman, *Augustus and the New Poetry*, Collection Latomus 88 (Brussels, 1967), "The Alexandrian Background," 31-60. For discussion of direct Callimachean influence on Latin poetry, see M. Puelma, "Die Vorbilder der Elegiendichtung in Alexandrien und Rom" *MusHel* 11 (1954) 101-16; W. Clausen, "Callimachus and Latin Poetry" *GRBS* 5 (1965) 181-96.

[3] Eventually both Horace and Propertius did try their hands at "Roman" poetry. Indeed, *Carm.* III. 1-6 and Prop. 3.1-5 are not only "Roman" but are closely related through imitation. *Cf.* W. R. Nethercut, "The Ironic Priest: Propertius' Roman Elegies *III*. 1-5: Imitations of Horace and Vergil" *AJP* 91 (1970) 385-407.

[4] The history of the *recusatio* poem in Rome has been minutely catalogued by W. Wimmel, *Kallimachos in Rom*, Hermes Einzelschr. 16 (1960). He says of *Aet.*-pref. 19-20: "für den neuen Zwiespalt wie geschaffene" (163). For detail on Callimachus and Propertius, see M. Hubbard, *Propertius* (London, 1974), "The Quest for Callimachus" 68-115.

their own talents. They decline to sing the praises of Caesar or other famous men because of lack of talent.[5] Callimachean poetry also provided Propertius and other Roman poets with the motif of Apollo warning the poet to keep away from epic and restrict himself to lighter genres.[6] The invoking of authority figures became a standard theme in Augustan poetry.[7]

Both of these motifs can be found in the Second and Third Books of Propertius. Propertian *recusatio* poems are uniformly serious, with a particular emphasis on the poet's lack of talent. Three of the six programmatic poems of Books II and III have lack of talent as their theme (2.1, 2.10, 3.9).[8] When we look for Propertian influence on Ovid's programmatic poems, we must bear this in mind. For Ovid is diametrically opposed to his predecessor in both of these ways. Ovid's programmatic poems are predominantly humorous,[9] and Ovid never, even under the guise of convention, denigrates his poetic abilities.

Yet Ovid was an Augustan poet, albeit a late one, and he could not dismiss the controversy entirely. He was clearly interested in Propertius' poetic reaction to the various pressures. All six of Ovid's programmatic poems show Propertian imitation, some of it quite extensive. It will become clear, however, that Ovid has undertaken his own program of reasons for writing love elegy. At times, his program borrows Callimachean or Propertian motifs but these are inevitably changed to fit his own purposes. *Am.* 1.1, 2.1, 2.18, 3.1, 1.15 and 3.15, read in that order, make the following points: 1) Ovid is writing love elegy because of the authority figure, Cupid, and because it is useful to him. Love elegy helps him win the hearts of girls. 2) He has the talent to write anything he wants, including epic which he has written in the past, and tragedy which he will write in the future. 3) The non-serious subject matter of the genre is no hindrance to his reputation. His love elegy has brought him immortality. The Propertian imitations which are skilfully woven

---

[5] *Cf.* Hor. *Carm.* 1.6, 2.12, 4.2, *Sat.* 2.1; Verg. *Ecl.* 6; Prop. 2.1.17 ff., 3.9.

[6] For a full discussion of this motif, *cf.* Wimmel (*supra*, note 4) 135-41.

[7] *E.g.*, Hor. *Carm.* 4.15; Prop. 3.3, 4.1.71 ff.; Verg. *Ecl.* 6.3-5; Ov. *Am.* 1.1, 3.1.

[8] The other programmatic poems are 2.34, 3.1 and 3.3. Prop. 4.1 is also a programmatic poem. There are no programmatic poems in Book I, although 1.7 and 1.9 contain elements which become important in Ovid's program.

[9] A good description of Ovid's humor in his programmatic poems is given by Reitzenstein (see Chapter I, note 9).

into all of these poems help emphasize these points. Furthermore, their often subtle and complex nature provides proof of the careful planning which must have preceded the actual writing of each of these elegies. They are by no means simple.

In the first poem of the *Amores*, Ovid very emphatically establishes Cupid as the authority figure responsible for his writing of love elegy.[10]

Am. 1.1.1-4:

Arma gravi numero violentaque bella parabam
    edere, materia conveniente modis.
par erat inferior versus; risisse Cupido
    dicitur atque unum surripuisse pedem.

Ovid begins his work by implying that he considers himself capable of writing serious, epic poetry.[11] He had, indeed, embarked upon that course when Cupid interfered and forced him to write elegy. Although the subject is treated in a light, jocular vein—the poem proceeds with Ovid arguing with Cupid about his interference in poetry—the importance of the subject elegy *vs.* epic is immediately apparent. Ovid has devoted the opening lines of the first poem of the *Amores* to explaining his defection from the ranks of the serious poets.

Prop. 3.3, which is the Propertian equivalent of this poem, i.e. a face-to-face encounter with an authority figure who orders the poet to write love elegy, is not found until fairly late in the corpus.[12] Propertius in that elegy meets two authority figures, Apollo (13-24) and the Muses, whose spokeswoman is Calliope (33-52). Apollo is, of course, the traditional Callimachean warning figure. Ovid by giving this role to Cupid, and a playful Cupid at that, has both

---

[10] Cupid as a poetic authority figure can also be seen in Prop. 2.13A. This, however, is only a brief (eight line) sketch. There is no philological evidence to suggest that Ovid's much more developed portrait of Cupid was directly borrowed from Prop. 2.13A.

[11] D. Kornzeniewski, "Ovids elegisches Proömium" *Hermes* 92 (1964) 182-213, points out that the first words of line 1 are meant to bring to mind the opening of the *Aeneid*. Ovid is thus dismissing not only the epic genre, but socially significant "Roman" epic.

[12] Neumann, 44-6, claims that *Am.* 1.1 is derived from Prop. 2.1 and that *Am.* 1.1.1-2 is a direct imitation of Prop. 2.1.41-2. Philological evidence is lacking.

introduced humor into this particular poem and told the reader much about the tone of his entire work.

We can be sure that this was a deliberate subversion of the serious, Apollo-warning-poet motif because of an imitation of Prop. 3.3.[13]

Prop. 3.3.41-2:

nil tibi sit rauco praeconia classica cornu
    flare, nec Aonium tingere Marte nemus.

Am. I.I.II-I2

crinibus insignem quis acuta cuspide Phoebum
    instruat, Aoniam Marte movente lyram?

The Propertian lines come from the speech which Calliope makes to the poet. Ovid, in lines whose context reminds the reader of the authority figure Calliope, has introduced Apollo, the other authority figure of Prop. 3.3. Both Propertian authority figures are thus subtly invoked by Ovid in his argument with Cupid. Yet it makes no difference. Cupid refuses to yield before the specter of Apollo and Calliope. The alert reader will read not only the surface meaning —Phoebus and Mars have their own spheres of influence—but will also see the contrast between the traditional staid poetic authority figures and Ovid's playful Cupid.

Indeed, Ovid reinforces the contrast of authority figures a few lines later when he says to Cupid:

an, quod ubique, tuum est? tua sunt Heliconia tempe?
    vix etiam Phoebo iam lyra tuta sua est?

                                        (*Am.* I.I.15-16)

The answer to the first two questions is yes. In the *Amores* Cupid is the god of poetry. He has been given this position because he does contrast so well with the traditional Apollo and he is thus capable of symbolizing the new spirit which characterizes the *Amores*.[14] Cupid was chosen for another reason also. The poet under his authority is in love and thus totally out of control of his own actions.

---

[13] Evidence of imitation here includes not only the . . . *Aoniam Marte* . . . of the pentameter line, but the repetition of the letter C in the hexameter.

[14] This lightness of tone has been viewed in a derogatory way. *E.g.*, B. Otis, "Ovid and the Augustans" *TAPA* 69 (1938) 188-229, claims Ovid is attempting "a *reductio ad absurdum* of the genre." (196).

This provides a perfect excuse for a poet involved in the serious *vs.* frivolous poetry controversy. Judging from *Am.* 1.1, 2.1 and 2.18, Ovid is not really responsible for his own actions.

These two themes—Cupid as the poetic authority figure and the victim-poet's total lack of control—are clearly demonstrated in *Am.* 1.2. While this elegy is not technically a programmatic poem, it is clearly of an introductory nature and expands upon the picture of Cupid we saw in *Am.* 1.1.[15] The main section of this poem is concerned with Ovid's description of Cupid's triumph where the poet himself marches as a captive in the procession (29-30). There has long been agreement that this triumph imagery is similar to the triumph Propertius describes in 3.1.[16] Only one Ovidian distich, however, is a definite imitation of Propertius.

Prop. 3.1.9-12:

quo me Fama levat terra sublimis, et a me
   nata coronatis Musa triumphat equis,
et mecum in curru parvi vectantur Amores,
   scriptorumque meas turba secuta rotas.

Am. 1.2.35-36:

Blanditiae comites tibi erunt Errorque Furorque,
   adsidue partes turba secuta tuas.

The point of the Propertian triumph is to show the control of the author over his material. The poet is triumphing, and indeed carries Love with him in his chariot. In 3.1 Propertius is under the sway of no authority figure. He is making his own poetic decisions.

How different the situation is in *Am.* 1.2! Love is in the chariot, the poet follows behind. The emphasis in the Ovidian elegy is on the poet's total lack of control over his situation. Error and Furor, two of the companions of the triumphing Cupid, are perfect symbols of this lack of control. That Cupid is once again a poetic authority figure is implied by *Blanditiae*, Cupid's third companion. While *blanditiae* is often used in the *Amores* to mean "sweet talk," in

---

[15] A. Cameron (Chapter I, note 18) feels that *Am.* 1.2 was originally the introductory poem to one of the five books of Ovid's first edition.

[16] *E.g.*, Neumann 24-26; Brandt (Chapter I, note 5) 43; P. Murgatroyd, "*Militia Amoris* and the Roman Elegists" *Latomus* 34 (1975) 59-79 claims that Propertius originated the poetical description of the triumph (70).

the programmatic poems it stands as a synonym for elegy.[17]
Cupid's triumph over Ovid thus shows not only the poet's lack of
control over himself, but also his lack of control over his poetry.
Am. 1.2 is a complete and total reversal of the situation in Prop. 3.1.

Once Love's poetic and emotional authority has been established,
Ovid is ready to proceed to the next phase of his programmatic
poetry. In the second book of the *Amores* Ovid offers another excuse
for his lack of interest in serious poetry. His new reason is expedien-
cy, or as he himself puts it, *clausit amica fores: ego cum Iove fulmen
omisi* (*Am.* 2.1.17). This does not mean that the authority figure
of Amor has been entirely omitted. The coercing Amor is introduced
in *Am.* 2.1 at line 3, and reintroduced in the last line of the poem:
carmina, purpureus quae mihi dictat Amor (2.1.38). This emphatic
position provides sufficient reminder of the importance Ovid
attached to this reason for writing elegy, even as Ovid proceeds to
offer additional excuses.

The utility argument which is paramount in both *Am.* 2.1 and
2.18 is a theme which was treated in some detail by Propertius in
1.7 and 1.9. Both elegies are imitated by Ovid in *Am.* 2.1 and
2.18.[18] In the Propertian poems, addressed to Ponticus, the poet
warns his friend to stop writing epic because it will be of no use to
him if he ever falls in love. Love poetry is the only genre that will
be able to help his suit with a girl. In 1.9, we see that Ponticus has
indeed fallen in love and Propertius is able to say, "I told you so."

Ovid turns these genial Propertian poems into weapons to be
used in the epic *vs.* elegy controversy. In so doing, he casts himself
in the role of Ponticus. In both 2.1 and 2.18 Ovid in the midst of
writing serious poetry is interrupted by Love and driven back to
elegy. The conflict between epic and elegy is apparent from the
very beginning of *Am.* 2.1.

---

[17] For the first meaning, see *Am.* 1.4.66; 2.19.17; 3.7.11, 58. In the programmatic poems, *cf.* 2.1.21:

blanditias elegosque levis, mea tela, resumpsi:
   mollierunt duras lenia verba fores.

Or 3.1.46, where Elegy herself is speaking:

quam tu non poteris duro reserare cothurno,
   haec est blanditiis ianua laxa meis.

[18] Neumann, 47-9, would base *Am.* 2.1 primarily on Prop. 2.1 although
he does see two parallels with Prop. 1.9. As regards *Am.* 2.18, Neumann
compares it to Prop. 1.7, concluding "mediam partem elegiae Ovidius
plane per se formavit, initio et conclusione Propertium imitatus." (89).

Am. 2.1.1-6:

Hoc quoque composui Paelignis natus aquosis
    ille ego nequitiae Naso poeta meae;
hoc quoque iussit Amor; procul hinc, procul este, severi:
    non estis teneris apta theatra modis.
me legat in sponsi facie non frigida virgo
    et rudis ignoto tactus amore puer.

Ovid first delineates the opposing sides in the controversy. In line three, *procul hinc, procul este, severi,* can hardly fail to remind the reader of Vergil *Aen.* 6.258, *procul o procul este, profani.* Then in line 5 Ovid imitates Propertius.

Prop. 1.7.13-14:[19]

me legat assidue post haec neglectus amator,
    et prosint illi cognita nostra mala.

This judicious use of imitation shows immediately where Ovid stands in the epic *vs.* elegy conflict. Ovid, like Propertius in 1.7, has alligned himself firmly with the elegiac genre.

The utility argument comes to the fore again later in *Am.* 2.1. By this time Ovid has explained his own particular situation, i.e. *clausit amica fores* (17). The word *fores* becomes the means by which Ovid links the usefulness of love elegy and the solution of his problems.

Am. 2.1.21-22:

blanditias elegosque levis, mea tela, resumpsi:
    mollierunt duras lenia verba fores.

Am. 2.1.27:

carminibus cessere fores, insertaque posti.

The force of these assertions is then increased by direct reference to Prop. 1.9.

---

[19] *Me legat* at the beginning of the hexameter line is important in establishing the imitation here. The poet showing preference for a particular audience by admonishing *me legat* is limited in Augustan poetry to these two places. Propertius, however, also offers the somewhat similar *quem legat* of 3.3.20.

Prop. 1.9.9-14:

quid tibi nunc misero prodest grave dicere carmen
   aut Amphioniae moenia flere lyrae?
plus in amore valet Mimnermi versus Homero:
   carmina mansuetus lenia quaerit Amor.
i quaeso et tristis istos compone libellos,
   et cane quod quaevis nosse puella velit.

Am. 2.1.29-34:

quid mihi profuerit velox cantatus Achilles?
   quid pro me Atrides alter et alter agent,
quique tot errando quot bello perdidit annos,
   raptus et Haemoniis flebilis Hector equis?
at facie tenerae laudata saepe puellae
   ad vatem, pretium carminis, ipsa venit.

Ovid has expanded Propertius' references to *grave carmen* and Homer into four lines of specific Homeric references, followed by a distich reiterating Propertius' idea of writing love elegy for practical reasons, to win a girl.

But this Propertian reference does more than merely emphasize how useful it is for someone in love to produce elegy. Propertius follows up this passage with a description of the general condition of Ponticus, the lover (15-32). This description makes it very clear that the lover is not in control of himself. Both the first and the last distichs stress this point.

Prop. 1.9.15-16:

quid si non esset facilis tibi copia? nunc tu
   insanus medio flumine quaeris aquam.

Prop. 1.9.31-32:

illis et silices et possint cedere quercus,
   nedum tu possis, spiritus iste levis.

Ovid wants to emphasize the lover's lack of control in both *Am.* 2.1 and 2.18, for in both poems he has embarked upon grand poetic schemes until Love—both the god and the emotion—forces him back to elegy. This, then, is another reason why Ovid chose to make extensive use of Prop. 1.7 and 1.9. in *Am.* 2.1 and 2.18.

These themes of utility, Love applying force to the poet, and lack of control once love comes, can all be seen again in the Propertian imitation at the beginning of *Am.* 2.18.[20]

Prop. 1.7.1-6:

Dum tibi Cadmeae dicuntur, Pontice, Thebae
    armaque fraternae tristia militiae,
atque, ita sim felix, primo contendis Homero,
    (sint modo fata tuis mollia carminibus:)
nos, ut consuemus, nostros agitamus amores,
    atque aliquid duram quaerimus in dominam.

Am. 2.18.1-4:

Carmen ad iratum dum tu perducis Achillem
    primaque iuratis induis arma viris,
nos, Macer, ignava Veneris cessamus in umbra,
    et tener ausuros grandia frangit Amor.

Although Ovid is addressing his friend, Macer, here, he himself is still playing the Ponticus role. He is the one who loses control when his girl sits on his lap (5-10). He is the one who gives up epic for elegy under the influence of love (11-12).

When we look at the rest of the poem, however, the themes of Amor and utility play a subordinate role. In both *Am.* 2.1 and 2.18 Ovid takes the position that he can write—and write well—in any genre he chooses. So in 2.18 Ovid claims to have been writing tragedy (13-18) when Love forced him back to the lighter genres,[21] a motif which finds a parallel in Ovid's venture into epic, also interrupted by Love, in *Am.* 2.1.11-16. Ovid is displaying his pride in his own talent, a talent which he views as unrestricted by genre. This contrasts sharply with the view of Propertius. In 1.7, Propertius says of himself:

---

[20] Neumann, 86, notes this imitation. He does not, however, view *Am.* 2.18 as a response to the serious *vs.* frivolous poetry controversy. He views the poem as a simple statement, "ut exponeret, quibus operibus eo tempore operam daret." (89).

[21] For a discussion of the dating of Ovid's various works based on *Am.* 2.18.13-34, see G. Luck, "Der Dichter zwischen Elegie und Epos" in W. Eisenhut (ed.), *Antike Lyrik* (Darmstadt, 1970), 464-79.

Prop. 1.7.21-24:

tum me non humilem mirabere saepe poetam,
    tunc ego Romanis praeferar ingeniis;
nec poterunt iuvenes nostro reticere sepulcro
    'Ardoris nostri magne poeta, iaces.'

While Propertius here is proud of his talent, he is also limiting his
sphere of activity to love elegy. Indeed, he establishes a clear
contrast between *ego* and *Romana ingenia* (22).

Ovid rejects not only Propertius' parochialism about elegy, but
also the conventional denigration of his own talent which Propertius makes a part of his second and third books. This is evident
from a Propertian imitation in *Am.* 2.1.[22]

Prop. 2.1.17-20:

quod mihi si tantum, Maecenas, fata dedissent,
    ut possem heroas ducere in arma manus,
non ego Titanas canerem, non Ossan Olympo
    impositam, ut caeli Pelion esset iter.

Am. 2.1.11-14:

ausus eram, memini, caelestia dicere bella
    centimanumque Gyen (et satis oris erat),
cum male se Tellus ulta est ingestaque Olympo
    ardua devexum Pelion Ossa tulit.

Ovid has directly contradicted one of Propertius' favorite conventions, the claim of meager poetic talent. Propertius in 2.1 goes on
to say that, if only he had the talent, he would sing of Caesar. Ovid,
in language and line structure designed to bring Propertius to mind,
claims that not only has he already written epic, it was good epic.
He is writing elegy at the moment not because of lack of talent,
but because of Amor and because of elegy's practical advantages.
The same theme reappears in 2.18 in regard to tragedy (13-18).

Ovid, then, in Book Two of the *Amores* has developed his programmatic poems along the lines of Prop. 1.7 and 1.9. The themes

---

[22] Neumann, 48, claims that each poet is simply using a conventional
topos. While it is true that this is a topos, the positions of the words *Olympo*
and *Pelion* as well as the parallel use of the parenthetical *Maecenas* and
memini indicate more specific imitation.

of external forces interrupting the attempt at serious poetry, the utility of love elegy, and the poet's pride in his talent are all found in these two Propertian elegies and used by Ovid in *Am.* 2.1 and 2.18.[23] The major difference between Ovid and his predecessor lies in Ovid's willingness to utilize his talents in genres other than elegy, even though he has temporarily alligned himself with the elegiac genre. The exploration of other genres is the theme that becomes most important in the programmatic poems of Ovid's third book.

Am. 3.1, the most complex of all of Ovid's programmatic poems, is the vehicle through which Ovid announces both his exploratory frame of mind and the impending end of his association with personal love elegy. Ovid made great use of Propertius when he was writing *Am.* 3.1, and in particular he imitated Prop. 3.3. In this elegy Propertius presents himself, the poet, being lectured by both Apollo and Calliope on how he should shun epic and continue writing elegy. Ovid constructs his poem differently—he presents the figures of Elegy and Tragedy debating each other—but the underlying problem is the same. In which genre shall the poet work?

Before the actual encounters begin, each poet carefully sets his scene. It is significant that Ovid borrows almost all of the accoutrements of his setting from the symbols furnished by Propertius in 3.3.

Am. 3.1.1-6:

Stat vetus et multos incaedua silva per annos;
    credibile est illi numen inesse loco.
fons sacer in medio speluncaque pumice pendens,
    et latere ex omni dulce queruntur aves.
hic ego dum spatior tectus nemoralibus umbris,
    quod mea, quaerebam, Musa moveret, opus.

---

[23] These themes are not limited to *Am.* 2.1 and 2.18. For example, if we return to *Am.* 1.1, we find a brief summary of the Ponticus story with Ovid, our erstwhile epic poet, taking the part of Ponticus:

'nec mihi materia est numeris levioribus apta,
    aut puer aut longas compta puella comas.'
questus eram, pharetra cum protinus ille soluta
    legit in exitium spicula facta meum
lunavitque genu sinuosum fortiter arcum
    'quod'que 'canas, vates, accipe' dixit 'opus.'

                      (*Am.* 1.1.19-24)

Most striking is Ovid's imitation of the cave.[24]

Prop. 3.3.27-28:

hic erat affixis viridis spelunca lapillis,
   pendebantque cavis tympana pumicibus.

Ovid has incorporated three of Propertius' exact words and at the same time taken over an important Propertian symbol of elegiac poetry. The use of water as the source of poetic inspiration and the theme of the Muses meeting the poet, were both common motifs in Greek and Latin poetry.[25] The symbol of a cave as the home of the Muses, though, seems to be entirely new with Propertius.[26]

Ovid's *fons sacer in medio* (3.1.3) is no doubt a reference to the water mentioned by Propertius in 3.3. Propertius, however, speaks of three separate sources, two within the cave and one outside of it (*Gorgoneus lacus*, l. 32; *Philitea aqua*, l. 52; *Bellerophontei ... umor equi*, l. 2). Two of these springs are sources of epic poetry. Only the *Philitea aqua* can be equated with elegy. Ovid leaves the exact nature of his spring undefined.[27] In addition, the birds mentioned by Ovid may correspond to the birds in Prop. 3.3.31-32:

   et Veneris dominae volucres, mea turba, columbae
      tingunt Gorgoneo punica rostra lacu.

The Propertian birds are important because they constitute a new symbol for elegy.[28] Yet interestingly enough, they are dipping their bills in the water of epic (*Gorgoneus lacus*) rather than elegy (*Philitea aqua*).

---

[24] Propertius has provided an elegant background for his poem through the use of epic language and in particular, through words taken over from Greek. In the course of four lines (27-30), we find the words *spelunca, tympana, orgia* (see Cordier, *Études sur la vocabulaire épique dans l'Énéide* [1939], 146-148, for their epic associations) and *calami* (see *ThLL* 3.124.1-25). In Ovid's introduction, *spelunca* is the only word which carries such epic overtones. Ovid uses it only four times in his entire corpus (*Met.* 10.692, 11.592, *Fast.* 1.555 and here). This would seem to indicate specific Propertian influence.

[25] See Wimmel (*supra*, note 4) 222-38.

[26] Wimmel, 244, says of Propertius' cave: "Grotte als neuer Symbolort des properzischen Dichtens, wo die Musen dem Dichter begegnen."

[27] Propertius, however, uses the word *fons* only in regard to the elegiac spring in the Cave of the Muses (3.3.51-52). It is possible that Ovid means the word *fons* to be a clue to the nature of his spring.

[28] Wimmel (*supra*, note 4) 242.

Ovid's imitation of Prop. 3.3 proceeds beyond the setting of the scene. Ovid also drew heavily on Propertius in his description of the authority figures presented in *Am.* 3.1. Propertius describes Apollo at line 14:

sic ait aurata nixus ad antra lyra.

Ovid varies this in his description of Tragedy to ... *pictis innixa cothurnis* (*Am.* 3.1.31). In addition, both figures carry something in their hands:

Prop. 3.3.25:

dixerat, et plectro sedem mihi monstrat eburno

Am. 3.1.13:

laeva manus sceptrum late regale movebat.

There is also a striking similarity in the first words each figure speaks to the poet: *quid tibi* (Prop. 3.3.15) and *ecquis erit tibi* (*Am.* 3.1.15). The correspondence between Elegy and Calliope is not so obvious, although both figures are renowned for their beauty. Propertius says of Calliope: *ut reor a facie, Calliopea fuit* (3.3.38). Ovid's Elegy exhibits the following characteristics: *forma decens, vestis tenuissima, vultus amantis* (*Am.* 3.1.9).

These close imitations of Prop. 3.3 all provide preparation for Ovid's decision at the end of *Am.* 3.1. Here he announces his intention to continue writing love elegy for a short time longer, even though he is becoming anxious to move on to more serious poetry. The poem concludes with the poet's prophetic remark, *a tergo grandius urguet opus* (3.1.70). This statement also prefigures the change in subject matter of the third book of the *Amores*. All of the poems in the first two books, with the exception of the programmatic poems, are concerned with love or courtship. In the third book, however, Ovid includes several elegies in which love is only a secondary theme.[29]

Ovid's use of serious elegy in his third book can be viewed as roughly parallel to the Roman elegy that Propertius attempts in Book IV. Ovid is working on a much smaller scale than Propertius but the general difference in tone between Books One and Two

---

[29] *Am.* 3.6 and 3.10 are essentially mythological narratives; 3.13 is an aetiological elegy on the Faliscan festival to Juno; 3.9 mourns the death of Tibullus. For a systematic treatment of Ovid's third book, see Chapter VI.

and Book Three of the *Amores* is readily apparent.[30] This desire to turn to a more serious type of elegy in Book III may have been a factor in Ovid's decision to use Prop. 3.3 so extensively in *Am.* 3.1. For Propertius in 3.3 is also hinting at his desire to write more serious elegy. This is indicated by the image of the doves, the symbols of elegy, noted above, who are dipping their bills in the *Gorgoneus lacus* (3.3.32), the Hippocrene, Ennius' source.[31] Propertius, then, has symbolically combined serious poetry and elegy. Since Apollo and Calliope in Prop. 3.3 restrict the poet to the elegiac genre, we can only look for elegy on weightier topics than those presented in Books I and II. Both the birds and the spring appear as part of the general background of *Am.* 3.1, from which we may reasonably assume that Ovid was capitalizing upon the complicated imagery of his predecessor. He, too, is about to write more serious elegy.[32]

In one sense, then, Ovid is eager to link his third book to the later elegy of Propertius. But just as in the programmatic poems of the second book, Ovid is very careful in *Am.* 3.1 to avoid denigrating his poetic talents. He deliberately disassociates himself from Propertius in this respect.

Prop. 4.1.57-58:

moenia namque pio coner disponere versu:
    ei mihi, quod nostro est parvus in ore sonus.

Am. 3.1.63-64:

altera me sceptro decoras altoque cothurno:
    iam nunc contacto magnus in ore sonus.

---

[30] It is generally agreed that both Ovid and Propertius arranged their elegies to reflect the progressive stages of their respective love affairs. So G. Williams (Chapter I, note 17) 514-15 says that Book I of each collection shows the early, happier stage of the relationship; Book II presents us with poems showing jealousy and strain; Book III shows the relationship at the breaking point. He sees only *Am.* 3.10 and 3.13 as parallel to Book IV of Propertius. *Am.* 3.9, he claims, finds its counterpart in Prop. 3.18.

[31] The nature of the spring is identified by W. Wimmel (*supra*, note 4) 242-43. W. R. Nethercut (*supra*, note 3) 392-93 points out the importance of the bird imagery for understanding Propertius' poetic goals.

[32] J. K. Newman (*supra*, note 1) 102-103 sees another clue to Ovid's impending change of tone. The use of the word *vates* at *Am.* 3.1.19 and 67 indicates Ovid's interest in poetry on a grand rather than trivial scale.

In 4.1 Propertius introduces his fourth book of elegy with the declaration that he is embarking on a different sort of poetry than that of his earlier books. He even presents himself as the Roman Callimachus (4.1.64). Yet in the midst of his assertions that he is about to write serious, Roman elegy, Propertius is still belittling his talent. Even when he is about to undertake his most serious poetry, he cannot admit publicly that he is creating something important. He is still restrained by the conventions of the epic *vs.* elegy controversy. Even serious elegy cannot lay claim to being more than *parvus sonus*.[33] Ovid's refutation of this Propertian line shows both his eagerness to avoid disparaging his poetic talent and his less parochial outlook about the genres in which he plans to write. *Magnus sonus* conveys a double meaning. It comments both on the quality of Ovid's work and on his choice of genre, in this case, tragedy. The *grandius opus* of line 70 thus prepares the reader not only for the serious elegy interspersed in Book III of the *Amores*, but for Ovid's ultimate departure from love elegy to work in more elevated genres.

In *Am.* 1.15 and 3.15 Ovid's pride in his talent reaches its zenith. Far from denigrating his poetic abilities, he now claims that his love elegy in and of itself will bring him overlasting fame and immortality. Prop. 3.1 expresses the same feeling of pride, but it is significant that Propertius carefully distinguishes between epic and elegiac poetry.[34] His fame, while tremendous, is limited to the latter category. Ovid in *Am.* 1.15, at least, demonstrates again the extent of his confidence in his talent. He views his love elegy as the equal of any poetry, whether light or serious.

Am. 1.15 shows imitation not only of Propertius but also of

---

[33] That Propertius is being conventional here is indicated by his next distich where he does express pride in his work:

sed tamen exiguo quodcumque e pectore rivi
  fluxerit, hoc patriae serviet omne meae.
                                                (4.1.59-60)

[34] For example, lines 15-18:

multi, Roma, tuas laudes annalibus addent,
  qui finem imperii Bactra futura canent.
sed, quod pace legas, opus hoc de monte Sororum
  detulit intacta pagina nostra via.

Propertius also begins and ends this poem with references to Callimachus. (In line 38, . . *Lycio*. . *deo* refers to Call. fr. 1.22. See W. A. Camps, *Propertius Elegies Book III* [Cambridge, 1966] *ad loc.*).

Horace, *Carm.* 3.30.[35] In the mid-section of the poem, Ovid lists a number of poets whose works have made them immortal (9-30). The imitations of Horace and Propertius are clustered at the beginning and end.

Carm. 3.30.1-7:

Exegi monumentum aere perennius
regalique situ pyramidum altius,
quod non imber edax, non Aquilo impotens
possit diruere aut innumerabilis
annorum series et fuga temporum
non omnis moriar multaque pars mei
vitabit Libitinam ...

Am. 1.15.1-8, 42:

Quid mihi, Livor edax, ignavos obicis annos
    ingeniique vocas carmen inertis opus,
non me more patrum, dum strenua sustinet aetas,
    praemia militiae pulverulenta sequi
nec me verbosas leges ediscere nec me
    ingrato vocem prostituisse foro?
mortale est, quod quaeris, opus; mihi fama perennis
    quaeritur, in toto semper ut orbe canar.

vivam, parsque mei multa superstes erit.

In addition to these imitations of Horace, *Am.* 1.15 contains two important imitations of Propertius. Lines 3-7, quoted above, are similar to Prop. 4.1.133-137:

    tum tibi pauca suo de carmine dictat Apollo
        et vetat insano verba tonare Foro.
    at tu finge elegos, fallax opus: haec tua castra!—
        scribat ut exemplo cetera turba tuo.
    militiam Veneris blandis patiere sub armis.

Philological evidence for imitation depends upon the specific words that appear in both passages; however, Ovid's refusal to become a

---

[35] These Horatian borrowings are easily recognized and have been noted by Neumann, 17-18; Brandt (Chapter I, note 5) *ad loc.*; F. Stoessl, "Ovids Lebensentscheidung" in *Festschrift K. Vrestska* (Heidelberg, 1970) 250-75, among others.

public speaker (6) and the military imagery (3-4) may also be direct borrowings from Propertius.

The other Propertian imitation appears at the end of *Am.* 1.15.

Prop. 3.1.21-24:

at mihi quod vivo detraxerit invida turba,
   post obitum duplici faenore reddet Honos;
omnia post obitum fingit maiora vetustas:
   maius ab exsequiis nomen in ora venit.

Am. 1.15.39-42:

pascitur in vivis Livor; post fata quiescit,
   cum suus ex merito quemque tuetur honos:
ergo etiam cum me supremus adederit ignis,
   vivam, parsque mei multa superstes erit.

The first two lines are obviously imitations. In the third line, Ovid's *supremus ignis* corresponds to Propertius' *exsequiae*.[36]

All of these imitations emphazise Ovid's point that poetry written in the lighter, less serious genres can provide immortality no less than epic or tragedy. The imitations of Horace fit easily into this framework. Horace has written three books of "light" lyric poetry and at the end can claim they are a permanent monument to him. Ovid, with perhaps greater confidence in himself, decides to make the same claim after only one book of love elegy. By imitating Horace, he is using the precedent set by the older poet to add weight to his own claim.

The imitation of Prop. 3.1 is of the same sort. It was mentioned earlier that Prop. 3.1 is the only elegy in which Propertius celebrates without restraint the glory of his elegy and the depth of his own talent. That Ovid would end his poem with an imitation from Prop. 3.1, then, is easily understandable. The Horatian imitation established the precedent of fame based on non-serious poetry. The Propertian imitation now establishes the precedent of fame derived specifically from the writing of love elegy.

The fame which love elegy can confer is brought out in a more

---

[36] Neumann, 17, recognizes this imitation, although he claims: "Ovidium, si ad totum carmen spectas, Horati III. 30 imitatum esse manifestum est." Neumann does not mention the imitation of Prop. 4.1.

subtle way by Ovid's imitation of Prop. 4.1.133-138. Horos is instructing Propertius:

> at tu finge elegos, fallax opus: haec tua castra!—
>   scribat ut exemplo cetera turba tuo.

$$(4.1.135\text{-}136)$$

From these lines we see that proof of fame depended partly on imitation.[37] Ovid, by imitating Propertius, has fashioned himself into one of the *cetera turba* and has put before us graphic proof of Propertius' fame as an elegist. Since the subject matter of *Am*. 1.15 is Ovid's fame as an elegist, the fame of Propertius, demonstrated by Ovid himself through imitation, is very pertinent to his argument that light poetry can and will bring him immortality.

This linking of fame with imitation continues in Ovid's list of famous Roman poets (19-30). The distichs describing Varro, Lucretius, Vergil, Tibullus and perhaps Gallus, all include recognizable imitations of the respective authors.[38] Missing from the list are Propertius and Horace, no doubt because they were still alive when Ovid wrote this poem. He is leading into his final theme —the immortal quality of poetic fame—by discussing only poets who are already dead.[39] Yet at the same time, he has carefully underlined the fame of both Horace and Propertius by his extensive imitations of their work. In *Am*. 1.15 Ovid is talking about fame on more than one level. Writing poetry will make one's name remembered, but it is also important to have one's fame acknowledged through imitation in the work of later poets.

In *Am*. 3.15, the last poem of the *Amores*, Ovid treats the theme of his own immortality in a much simpler manner. He once again claims that his love elegy is sufficient to guarantee his fame even though he has now decided to abandon elegy for more elevated genres (17-18). In this poem, Ovid contrasts himself with Propertius through specific imitations of Prop. 4.1.

----

[37] The same theme plays a part in Prop. 3.1:

scriptorumque meas turba secuta rotas (12).

[38] See Stoessl (*supra*, note 36) 258-61. In the case of Gallus, he recognizes the similarity of *Am*. 1.15.29 to Prop. 2.3.43 and then ventures the opinion that both of these lines may be imitations of a formula used by Gallus (261). Barsby (Chapter I, note 5) 161-63 also discusses the allusions contained in these lines.

[39] Horace died in 8 B.C., Tibullus and Vergil in 19 B.C. This would mean, if my analysis is correct, that Prop. 4.1 was available to Ovid before 8 B.C.

Prop. 4.1.63-70:

ut nostris tumefacta superbiat Umbria libris,
    Umbria Romani patria Callimachi!
scandentis quisquis cernit de vallibus arces,
    ingenio muros aestimet ille meo!
Roma, fave, tibi surgit opus, date candida cives
    omina, et inceptis dextera cantet avis!
sacra diesque canam et cognomina prisca locorum:
    has meus ad metas sudet oportet equus.

Am. 3.15.11-14:

atque aliquis spectans hospes Sulmonis aquosi
    moenia, quae campi iugera pauca tenent,
'quae tantum' dicet 'potuistis ferre poetam,
    quantulacumque estis, vos ego magna voco.'

Am. 3.15.2:

raditur haec elegis ultima meta meis.

Am. 3.15 is Ovid's final expression of pride in the *Amores*. He views it as a work sufficient in itself to provide him with eternal fame. Although he will proceed to more serious poetry, he doesn't have to. His *meta* has already been reached (2); the *Amores* are no shame to him (4). Ovid's pride in his work becomes even more pronounced because of the comparison with Prop. 4.1. In this elegy Propertius states his desire to become the Roman Callimachus. Serious elegy is his new goal and it is on that that his fame will be based. This statement carries an implicit denigration of the poetry Propertius has already produced. It is this denigration of love elegy that Ovid refuses to accept. Through imitation he has directly contradicted his predecessor.

Am. 3.15 is the last poem of the *Amores*. It is significant, then, that in the last six lines of this poem Ovid has summarized the three main themes which have been discussed in this chapter.

Am. 3.15.15-20:

culte puer puerique parens Amathusia culti,
    aurea de campo vellite signa meo;
corniger increpuit thyrso graviore Lyaeus:
    pulsanda est magnis area maior equis.
inbelles elegi, genialis Musa, valete,
    post mea mansurum fata superstes opus.

Love as the authority figure who forces the poet to write elegy, Ovid's confidence that his talent is sufficient for any genre of poetry, pride in his love elegy even though it is light, non-serious poetry— these are the themes so important in Ovid's programmatic poems. While the programmatic poems of Propertius are very different, we have seen that Ovid nevertheless made extensive and often subtle use of them in the development of his own programmatic themes.

CHAPTER THREE
PARODY

The term parody has been applied by some scholars to the entire *Amores*.[1] Such a judgment must be based upon the general difference in tone between Ovid's elegy and that of his predecessors, the contrast between the light and playful and the sober and intense. While this may qualify as parody by modern definition, it does not meet the stricter ancient standards. Cicero and Quintilian agree in defining parody as humor created through the use of recognizable imitation.[2] Modern studies have shown the importance of context in creating this humor.[3] A less serious context or a humbler subject is mandatory for true parody.[4] The humor is derived from the conflict of the reader's associations, for the new context jars when compared to the old.

In order to use parody, then, an author must wish to gain a non-serious, humorous effect. Since this is precisely the tone which Ovid adopts most often in the *Amores*, his opportunities to parody his predecessors are legion. Indeed, parody seems to have been a hallmark of Ovid's work in general, for Quintilian mentions Ovid by name as a parodist.[5] Macer is the object of parody mentioned

---

[1] *E.g.*, J. P. Sullivan, "Two Problems in Roman Love Elegy" *TAPA* 92 (1961) 522-536: "Ovid represents a debasement of the elegiac tradition, he is a parody of his predecessors, not representative of them" (535). I. M. DuQuesnay (Chapter I, note 13): "None the less the *persona* which Ovid adopts in the poems is clearly a parody of Propertius" (7).

[2] Cic. *De Or.* II.54.257:

Saepe etiam versus facete interponitur, vel ut est, vel paulum immutatus, aut aliqua pars versus.

Quint. *Inst. Or.* VI.3.96-7:

Adiuvant urbanitatem et versus commode positi, seu toti ut sunt ... seu verbis ex parte mutatis ... seu ficti notis versibus similes, quae παρῳδία dicitur.

[3] See F. J. Lelièvre, "The Basis of Ancient Parody," *G. and R.*, 2nd ser. I (1954) 66-81; J. P. Cèbe, *La caricature et la parodie dans le monde romain antique des origines à Juvenal* (Paris, 1966) 284-335; J.-M. Frécaut, *L'esprit et l'humour chez Ovide* (Grenoble, 1972) 114-24.

[4] One example is *Catalepton* 10, a parody of Cat. 4. The terms Catullus affectionately applies to his ship are used in the later poem to describe a muleteer. For a detailed description, see R. E. H. Westendorp Boerma, *P. Vergili Maronis Catalepton*, Vol. 2 (Assen, 1963) 31-38. One also thinks of the parodies of Vergil cited by Donatus (*Vita* 174 ff.).

[5] Quint. *Inst. Or.* VI.3.96.

by Quintilian, but by definition, any serious poet would do.[6] In the *Amores*, then, we would expect Ovid to parody the most serious of his predecessors, Propertius.[7] Ovid does not disappoint us in this, but he does limit both the amount and the subject matter of the Propertian parody which he includes in the *Amores*. Generally, Ovid keeps his parody short—one or at most two distichs—and includes only one Propertian parody per poem. His favorite subjects for parody are things which Propertius took very seriously. In the *Amores* we find parody of Augustus and his programs, one of which was the promotion of serious, Roman literature. The greater part of Ovid's parody, however, has as its subject the Propertian view of the lover and the trials and tribulations which he must endure at the hands of his mistress.

Ovid's most blatant use of parody concerning Augustus can be seen at the end of *Am*. 1.2. Ovid's poem begins with a description of the symptoms of love that have struck the poet and then develops into a detailed description of Cupid's triumph in which Ovid himself will participate as *praeda recens* (1.2.29). The poem ends with the following appeal to Cupid:

Am. 1.2.49-52:

ergo cum possim sacri pars esse triumphi,
    parce tuas in me perdere victor opes.
aspice cognati felicia Caesaris arma:
    qua vicit, victos protegit ille manu.

---

[6] One example should suffice. The *Ars*, Ovid's humorous didactic poem, offers many opportunities for parody of Lucretius. Lucretius at one point is attempting to prove that all things are made up of bodies too small to be seen.

Lucr. 1.312-314:
anulus in digito subter tenuatur habendo,
stilicidi casus lapidem cavat, uncus aratri
ferreus occulte decrescit vomer in arvis.

Ars 1.473-477:
ferreus adsiduo consumitur anulus usu,
    interit adsidua vomer aduncus humo.
quid magis est saxo durum, quid mollius unda?
    dura tamen molli saxa cavantur aqua.
Penelopen ipsam, persta modo, tempore vinces.

Ovid is also "proving" something: if you persevere in your suit, you will eventually wear down the woman's resistence and gain your end.

[7] This is not to imply that Propertius did not have his light and jocular moments. E. Lefèvre, *Propertius Ludibundus* (Heidelberg, 1966) has demonstrated the place of humor in Propertian elegy.

The last two lines of this passage have been closely modelled on a Propertian distich which the manuscripts give as part of 2.16.[8]

Prop. 2.16.41-42:

Caesaris haec virtus et gloria Caesaris haec est:
 illa, qua vicit, condidit arma manu.

Propertius' tone is very solemn, for he is intent on paying a sincere compliment to Augustus. Ovid's imitation, however, is much less serious. He is using Caesar as an example for his captor, Amor. The playfulness of Ovid's tone becomes even more obvious by the fact that Caesar is not even treated in his own right but in the capacity of a relative of Cupid.

Many scholars have felt that Propertius' compliment to Caesar is out of place at 2.16.41-42 and have suggested new contexts.[9] The distich fits most appropriately, however, in a position following Prop. 3.11.50.[10] 3.11 is Propertius' Cleopatra poem and the context is certainly suitable for a remark about Augustus' clemency. In addition, if this transposition is accepted, Ovid's parody of Propertius can be extended from two lines to four. Prop. 3.11.49-52 would then read:

              ... cape, Roma, triumphum
 et longum Augusto salva precare diem!
Caesaris haec virtus et gloria Caesaris haec est:
 illa, qua vicit, condidit arma manu.

Am. 1.2.49-52 also mentions a triumph only it is the mock triumph of Cupid in which the poet himself must take part as a captive. Ovid follows this with a prayer to Cupid to spare him. This corresponds to Propertius' much more serious statement that Rome should pray for long life for Augustus. Even though the contrast

---

[8] Neumann, 12-13, recognizes this imitation but claims that Ovid, like Propertius, is paying a sincere compliment to Caesar.

[9] A. E. Housman, for example, would place it following 3.11.38 (see his "Emendationes Propertianae," *JP* 16 [1888] 10). Butler favors a position following 3.22.22 (see Barber [Chapter I, note 1] 54). Those who believe the lines are not out of place include D. R. Shackleton Bailey, *Propertiana* (Cambridge, 1956) 96-97; P. J. Enk (Chapter 1, note 5: *Liber Secundus*, part 2) 243.

[10] For detailed arguments, see K. Berman, "A Note on Propertius 2.16.41-42" *CP* 66 (1971) 110-12.

between Prop. 3.11.49-50 and *Am.* 1.2.49-50 is less specific than that of the two distichs praising Caesar, Ovid, by insinuating that Rome's triumph over Cleopatra is in some way analogous to Cupid's triumph over him, has certainly created parody.[11]

Ovid's playful treatment of Augustus continues indirectly in his parody of a Propertian distich that upholds an important Augustan ideal. The virtues of the simple, austere life were evidently much touted by the emperor.[12] While many authors of the period at least paid lip service to this ideal, Ovid never bothered. At one point in the *Ars* he states:

> prisca iuvent alios, ego me nunc denique natum
>   gratulor: haec aetas moribus apta meis.
>
> (3.121-122)

When he wrote the *Amores*, Ovid was not yet showing open opposition. However, this same attitude can be seen in a subtler form.

Prop. 2.16.19-20:

atque utinam Romae nemo esset dives, et ipse
    straminea posset dux habitare casa!

Am. 2.9.17-18:

Roma, nisi inmensum vires promosset in orbem,
    stramineis esset nunc quoque tecta casis.[13]

The Propertian distich is a wish for a simpler, less luxurious (and

---

[11] In addition to this specific Propertian parody, the structural parallelism between *Am.* 1.2 and Prop. 3.11 may suggest that Ovid modelled his entire poem on the Propertian elegy. Each poem begins with a four line question about love which the poet then proceeds to answer (5-8). Next come lists of examples (Prop. 3.11.9-28; *Am.* 1.2.9-18). The major part of each elegy is a lengthy narrative. Propertius describes the evil nature of Cleopatra and her plots against Rome (3.11.29-56). Ovid, in a much lighter vein, describes Cupid's triumph (1.2.19-42). Finally, both elegies end with the mention of a god, followed by an invocation. Propertius names Apollo (69) and then invokes an unknown sailor (71-72). Ovid mentions Bacchus (47) and invokes Cupid (49-52).

[12] Augustus, for example, insisted that the women of his household learn and practice spinning and weaving, symbols of old-fashioned feminine virtue. (See Suet. *Aug.* 64.)

[13] The adjective *stramineus* is used only twice by Ovid, here and at *Fast.* 5.631. Ovid's choice of this word, his coupling of it with *casis*, the position the two words occupy in his distich, all indicate Propertian imitation.

by implication, less decadent) life style at Rome. The fact that Propertius has included Augustus within his wish in a statement which may be construed as complimentary may reflect the older elegist's connection with the regime.[14] Propertius uses these lines in a very serious context. Cynthia has become enamoured with a rich praetor and the poet is bemoaning his exclusion from her company.

Ovid has completely reversed Propertius' sentiment. The implication of his distich is that a life of austerity is bad, a life of luxury is good. In addition, he has created parody by placing the serious Propertian wish in a context where we can hardly take him seriously. In *Am.* 2.9 Ovid is pleading with Cupid to release him from love's soldiery. While much of the appeal is serious, this particular distich is simply an afterthought.

Am. 2.9.15-18:

tot sine amore viri, tot sunt sine amore puellae:
   hinc tibi cum magna laude triumphus eat.
(Roma, nisi inmensum vires promosset in orbem,
   stramineis esset nunc quoque tecta casis.)

All of the military glory of Rome has been reduced to an argument aimed at Cupid. By conquering people who are as yet undefeated, Cupid, like Rome, can extend his rule. The humor of this treatment is both obvious and intentional.

Literary pretensions, or specifically, a preference for writing poetry more serious than love elegy are also parodied by Ovid in the *Amores*. Serious interest in Propertius' response to the epic *vs.* elegy conflict is concentrated in Ovid's programmatic poems.[15] Elsewhere in the *Amores* Ovid does not hesitate to parody the very subject he treated seriously in these programmatic poems. The elegies in which such parody is found, however, are not those whose primary subject is poetry. The Propertian imitations provide casual, humorous decoration for the poems in which they appear. They should not be taken as part of Ovid's statement of his poetic program.

---

[14] The compliment here evolves around the verb *posset*. Propertius seems to be saying that at the moment Augustus cannot live the simple life. It is not that he would not like to do so. See P. J. Enk (Chapter 1, note 5: *Liber Secundus*, part 2) 236.

[15] This has been discussed in detail, *supra*, Chapter II.

The best example can be found in *Am.* 2.6, Ovid's humorous lament over Corinna's dead parrot. Ovid has included within this elegy an imitation from Prop. 3.3, the important programmatic poem in which the poet is instructed by Apollo and the Muses.

Prop. 3.3.31-32:

et Veneris dominae volucres, mea turba, columbae
   tingunt Gorgoneo punica rostra lacu.

Am. 2.6.21-22:

tu poteras fragiles pinnis hebetare zmaragdos
   tincta gerens rubro Punica rostra croco.

Birds are, of course, an important element in *Am.* 2.6. But these particular Propertian birds not only appear in the context of an extremely serious poem, they themselves constitute an important symbol of elegy, elegy which will treat serious subjects.[16] Ovid by equating Corinna's dead pet with these important Propertian literary symbols has created an obvious parody. We have moved from the sublime to the ridiculous with particularly humorous results.[17]

A similar imitation can be seen at *Am.* 2.5.37-38, where Ovid has parodied Prop. 2.34, the long programmatic poem addressed to Lynceus.

Prop. 2.34.51-52:

harum nulla solet rationem quaerere mundi,
   nec cur fraternis Luna laboret equis.

Am. 2.5.37-38, 41-42:

quale rosae fulgent inter sua lilia mixtae
   aut, ubi cantatis, Luna, laborat equis; . . .
his erat aut alicui color ille simillimus horum,
   et numquam casu pulchrior illa fuit.

In 2.34 Propertius is advising his friend, newly struck down by love, about the usefulness of writing love elegy rather than more

---

[16] See Chapter II, pages 18-20.

[17] For a discussion of what *Am.* 2.6 owes to Catullus 3 see Frécaut (*supra*, note 3) 179, 343-45.

serious, scholarly poetry. One of his phrases for learned poetry is
... *Luna laboret equis*.[18] Ovid has imitated this in his pentameter
but in so doing has moved the phrase to a much different and
lighter context. Instead of describing learned poetry, Ovid is
describing the blush on the face of his girl when he accuses her of
flirting at a party. The incongruity of the phrase in Ovid's context
creates humor.

The remaining instances of Propertian parody in the *Amores* are
concerned with love or the lover. Ovid is particularly prolific in
parodying Propertius' intense and serious attitude about all of the
little trials of love. Specific imitations of his predecessor very clearly
show the difference between the Propertian view of love and the
Ovidian. Ovid does not even attempt in the *Amores* to create a
sustained impression of sincerity and passion.[19] Playfulness and
gamesmanship predominate.

A good example of this contrast in attitude can be found in
Am. 3.3, where Ovid is working with the traditional motif of the
lover swearing by his eyes.[20] He has closely imitated Propertius.

Prop. 1.15.33-38:

tam tibi ne viles isti videantur ocelli,
    per quos saepe mihi credita perfidia est!
hos tu iurabas, si quid mentita fuisses,
    ut tibi suppositis exciderent manibus:
et contra magnum potes hos attollere Solem,
    nec tremis admissae conscia nequitiae?

These lines are introduced into a serious context. Cynthia has sworn
falsely many times, and Propertius wonders that she does not tremble
in fear at her own perjury. The tone of Propertius' elegy is one of
despair over Cynthia's lack of faith. Despair eventually gives way to
bitterness as Propertius cautions in his final lines:

---

[18] The moon and the various natural phenomena connected with it
were a traditional topic for learned poetry in Latin. See, *e.g.*, Verg. *G.* 2.478,
Aen. 1.742; Tib. 2.4.18; Sil. 14.39.

[19] For a discussion of the whole question of "sincerity" in elegy, see
A. W. Allen, " 'Sincerity' and the Roman Elegists" *CP* 45 (1950) 145-160.
Propertius only is discussed by E. Reitzenstein, "Wirklichkeitsbild und
Gefühlsentwicklung bei Properz" *Philologus*, Supp. 29, Heft II (Leipzig,
1931).

[20] For examples, see Rothstein (Chapter I, note 5) *ad loc.*

Prop. 1.15.41-42:

quis ego nunc pereo, similis moniturus amantis
  'O nullis tutum credere blanditiis!'

Ovid has imitated the first two lines of this Propertian passage.[21]

Am. 3.3.9-14:

argutos habuit: radiant ut sidus ocelli,
  per quos mentita est perfida saepe mihi.
scilicet aeterni falsum iurare puellis
  di quoque concedunt, formaque numen habet.
perque suos illam nuper iurasse recordor
  perque meos oculos: et doluere mei.

He is also complaining about his girl's lack of faith and her false swearing, but the tone of this elegy is completely different. Ovid's accusations are hardly serious and bitter. He has parodied the conventional motif by creating a ludicrous situation. Corinna has done the false swearing, but Ovid's eyes are the ones that hurt. Thus at the end of *Am.* 3.3, we find humor, not bitterness.

Am. 3.3.47-48:

tu tamen illorum moderatius utere dono,
  aut oculis certe parce, puella, meis.

The second attitude which Ovid parodies in the *Amores* is the preference for a spirited girl friend. Propertius seems to enjoy it when Cynthia quarrels with him, and, indeed, goes so far as to write a detailed description of one of their fights (4.8). In this poem Cynthia is termed, *non operosa comis, sed furibunda decens* (4.8.52). The theme is also treated in Prop. 3.8, which begins:

Dulcis ad hesternas fuerat mihi rixa lucernas.

To Propertius, quarrels were evidently a sign of love (3.8.19). Near the end of 3.8 he states:

---

[21] In addition to the similarity between Prop. 1.15.34 and *Am.* 3.3.10, Propertian influence may be indicated by Ovid's use of *ocelli*. Propertius in his first book always chooses *ocellus* over *oculus*. In the third book of the *Amores*, however, Ovid shows no such decided preference. In fact, *oculi* is used more frequently (eleven times, to seven for *ocelli*).

Prop. 3.8.27-34:

odi ego quae numquam pungunt suspiria somnos:
  semper in irata pallidus esse velim.
dulcior ignis erat Paridi, cum Graia per arma
  Tyndaridi poterat gaudia ferre suae:
dum vincunt Danai, dum restat barbarus Hector,
  ille Helenae in gremio maxima bella gerit.
aut tecum aut pro te mihi cum rivalibus arma
  semper erunt: in te pax mihi nulla placet.

Ovid has imitated this passage at the end of *Am.* 2.19.[22]

Am. 2.19.55-60:

nil metuam? per nulla traham suspiria somnos?
  nil facies, cur te iure perisse velim?
quid mihi cum facili, quid cum lenone marito?
  corrumpit vitio gaudia nostra suo.
quin alium, quem tanta iuvet patientia, quaeris?
  me tibi rivalem si iuvat esse, veta.

Parody here has been created more by a change of object than by
change of context. Propertius wants his girl friend to react angrily.
Ovid wants the same reaction from his girl friend's husband. This
man should experience more jealous and angry feelings which would
lead him to guard his wife more closely. Only with an element of
danger present does Ovid feel that he can obtain true pleasure from
the affair. Ovid finally says to the man, *lentus es et pateris nulli
patienda marito* (2.19.51). Propertius, on the other hand, in 3.8 has
stated, *hostibus eveniat lenta puella meis* (20). Both poets are agreed
on the benefits of an angry reaction. The difference (and the
parody) lies in the people from whom they want to elicit this
reaction.

The parody continues in *Am.* 2.19.59-60. That Ovid was modelling
this distich on Prop. 3.8.33-34 can be seen from the number of
words the two couplets have in common. In addition, it should be
noted that *Am.* 2.19.59-60 are the final lines of Ovid's poem. Some

---

[22] The similarity of the last four words of Prop. 3.8.27 and *Am.* 2.19.55
indicates imitation. Ovid, however, has eliminated Propertius' unconven-
tional verb *pungunt* and substituted *traham*. Ovid, like all the Augustan
poets except Propertius, never uses the verb *pungo*.

scholars have also concluded that Prop. 3.8 should end at line 34.[23]
If we accept this, we have still another parallel, i.e. the end of
Am. 2.19 echoing the end of Prop. 3.8. In any event, the same kind
of parody is still operating. Both poets again seek quarrels. The
Propertian quarrels will be with unnamed rivals, presumably
attracted to Cynthia because of her beauty, or else they will be
quarrels with Cynthia herself. Ovid again wants his quarrels and
rivalry to involve his girl friend's husband. The lack of difficulty in
his liaison is not at all pleasing to him. This unique twist—the
change of object from girl friend to girl friend's husband—gives
humor to Ovid's poem and at the same time shows how different
the playful attitude of Ovid is from the intensity of Propertius.

The hot tempered Propertian girl friend is parodied a second
time in the *Amores*, but with a different emphasis. Through direct
imitation Ovid compares the reasons for Propertius' nighttime
bravery with the reasons for his own.

Prop. 3.16.5-10:

quid faciam? obductis committam mene tenebris,
    ut timeam audaces in mea membra manus?
at si distulero haec nostro mandata timore,
    nocturno fletus saevior hoste mihi.
peccaram semel, et totum sum pulsus in annum:
    in me mansuetas non habet illa manus.

Am. 1.6.9-14:

at quondam noctem simulacraque vana timebam;
    mirabar, tenebris quisquis iturus erat:
risit, ut audirem, tenera cum matre Cupido
    et leviter 'fies tu quoque fortis' ait.
nec mora, venit amor: non umbras nocte volantis,
    non timeo strictas in mea fata manus.

Propertius' fear of travelling Rome's streets at night is surpassed
by his fear of his mistress' tears and recriminations. The hands of
the robbers may be *audaces* but the hands of Cynthia are *non
mansuetas*. The girl friend's temper is a force to be reckoned with.

---

[23] Most notably, Postgate. For arguments on the question, see D. R.
Shackleton Bailey (*supra*, note 9) 157-58. Shackleton Bailey would omit
lines 35-36 but retain lines 37-40 as part of 3.8.

Ovid is also describing his fear of going out at night. His trepidation has been overcome, however, not by thoughts of the fiery temper of a specific girl friend, but because Cupid has made him brave. The whole episode has a light, jocular quality. *Risit* and *leviter* are used by Ovid to describe Cupid; *saevior hoste* is Propertius' description of Cynthia. Therein lies the parody. To Propertius the bondage of love, manifested here in the need to submit himself to dangers, is closely linked to the temper of a specific girl. Propertius fears Cynthia's anger. To Ovid no specific girl matters. The state of being in love—not fear of recriminations—makes him brave. It is part of the role of lover to brave the terrors of the night in pursuit of pleasure. While Ovid plays this role with gusto, he carefully points out through imitation that the demanding relationship with one specific woman is not necessary for his enjoyment of love. The hot-tempered Cynthia has become Ovid's calm, smiling figure of Cupid.

Ovid's more detached tone, his view of love as a game, is clearly shown twice more through imitation which parodies Propertius. In both imitations, Ovid contrasts his own view of a successful love affair with that of Propertius and insinuates, by changing the context of the imitation, that Propertius took the trials of love too seriously. In both imitations, Ovid actually welcomes the trials that Propertius found so onerous. To the younger elegist these problems serve to add spice to his affair.

The first imitation treats the problem of the lover's access to his mistress.

Prop. 2.4.1-4:

Multa prius dominae delicta queraris oportet,
    saepe roges aliquid, saepe repulsus eas,
et saepe immeritos corrumpas dentibus unguis,
    et crepitum dubio suscitet ira pede!

Am. 2.9b.43-46: [24]

me modo decipiant voces fallacis amicae
    (sperando certe gaudia magna feram),
et modo blanditias dicat, modo iurgia nectat;
    saepe fruar domina, saepe repulsus eam.

---

[24] Neumann, 8, says that Ovid is not deliberately imitating Propertius here. He bases his opinion on the different attitudes manifested in the two elegies. This is, of course, precisely the reason why I think Ovid was imitating Propertius.

Propertius in 2.4 is complaining of the hardships the lover must
endure at the hands of his mistress. He speaks with a great deal of
bitterness. In fact, at the end of 2.4, he is ready to abandon heterosexual love altogether, or so he claims, since boys are so much
easier to understand.

Prop. 2.4.17-18: [25]

hostis si quis erit nobis, amet ille puellas:
    gaudeat in puero, si quis amicus erit.

The context of *Am.* 2.9b is just the opposite of Prop. 2.4. Ovid
is reaffirming his desire for love and speaking of the trials Propertius
would banish as positive forces which only add to his enjoyment.
This opposition to Propertius continues to the end of the elegy. For
Ovid ends *Am.* 2.9b with a strong affirmation of the desirability
of heterosexual love.

Am. 2.9b.51-54:

si tamen exaudis, pulchra cum matre, rogantem,
    indeserta meo pectore regna gere:
accedant regno, nimium vaga turba, puellae;
    ambobus populis sic venerandus eris.

It is difficult not to see this last couplet as Ovid's answer to Prop.
2.4.17-18, particularly in view of the similar words which end the
lines. The joys of heterosexual love are clearly emphasized by
Ovid's use of *ambobus populis*. Propertius has separated the girls
from the boys, but Ovid reunites the sexes in their veneration
of Cupid.

A similar parody can be found in *Am.* 3.4.

Prop. 2.23.19-20:

nec dicet 'Timeo, propera iam surgere, quaeso:
    infelix, hodie vir mihi rure venit.'

Am. 3.4.31-32:

indignere licet, iuvat inconcessa voluptas:
    sola placet, 'timeo' dicere si qua potest.

---

[25] For a review of the problems regarding the arrangement of the lines in
Prop. 2.4, see Shackleton Bailey (*supra*, note 9) 68-69; Butler and Barber
(Chapter I, note 5) *ad loc.*

Both poets are discussing the kind of girl who is most pleasing. Propertius after enumerating all of the problems involved in carrying on trysts with freeborn, married women opts for love with prostitutes. Ovid, on the other hand, claims that difficulties of access only enhance desire. Once again Ovid presents himself as the less involved, more sophisticated lover.

This imitation and the parody which it creates are generally recognized by scholars.[26] Indeed, this is the only place in the *Amores* where Ovid directly quotes Propertius. The parody, however, does not end with this one distich. The structure of the end of *Am.* 3.4 indicates that Ovid composed the last eighteen lines of his elegy with Prop. 2.23 in mind.

Prop. 2.23.13-22:

contra, reiecto quae libera vadit amictu,
   custodum et nullo saepta timore, placet.
cui saepe immundo Sacra conteritur Via socco,
   nec sinit esse moram, si quis adire velit;
differet haec numquam, nec poscet garrula, quod te
   astrictus ploret saepe dedisse pater,
nec dicet 'Timeo, propera iam surgere, quaeso:
   infelix, hodie vir mihi rure venit.'
et quas Euphrates et quas mihi misit Orontes,
   me iuerint: nolim furta pudica tori.

The point of the Propertian passage is to convince the reader that foreign prostitutes are preferable to married Roman women as sexual partners. The prostitute is truly free (13). Propertius bolsters his argument by invoking both authority figures and morality in general. A lover who insists on a married woman must deal with his own father when the woman demands gifts (18), her husband (20) and social disapproval (*furta pudica tori*, 22).

Ovid devotes the end of *Am.* 3.4 to dismantling the Propertian argument point by point. He begins with the imitation noted above —fear is what adds spice to the tryst. Next he answers Propertius' argument that the foreign prostitute is unguarded and can come and go as she pleases.

---

[26] See, *e.g.*, Neumann, 22; Rothstein (Chapter I, note 5) *ad loc.*; Brandt (Chapter I, note 5) *ad loc.*

Am. 3.4.33-36:

nec tamen ingenuam ius est servare puellam;
hic metus externae corpora gentis agat.
scilicet ut possit custos 'ego' dicere 'feci',
in laudem servi casta sit illa tui? [27]

Ovid then heaps scorn upon the figure of the stern and disapproving husband, and abolishes the specter of social disapproval.

Am. 3.4.37-40, 43-44:

rusticus est nimium, quem laedit adultera coniunx,
et notos mores non satis Urbis habet,
in qua Martigenae non sunt sine crimine nati
Romulus Iliades Iliadesque Remus. . . .
si sapis, indulge dominae vultusque severos
exue nec rigidi iura tuere viri.

But perhaps the cleverest parody of all is the one which Ovid creates from the Propertian complaint about gifts. Propertius, speaking from the position of the poor lover, emphasizes the figure of the father from whom the money for presents must be procured. Ovid emphasizes the more pleasant prospects of friends and banquets.

Am. 3.4.45-48:

et cole quos dederit (multos dabit) uxor amicos:
gratia sic minimo magna labore venit;
sic poteris iuvenum convivia semper inire
et, quae non dederis, multa videre domi.

Ovid's *tour de force* is accomplished by a change in the point of view. We now see gift-giving from the vantage point of the agreeable, cuckolded husband. Extra marital affairs will work to his advantage, as well as to the advantage of the wife and her lover.[28]

The end of *Am.* 3.4 provides a clear example of Ovid's light,

---

[27] In composing this passage, Ovid may also have been influenced by Prop. 2.23.3-4, where the contrast between *ingenuus* and *servus* is specifically expressed.

[28] I.M. Le M. Du Quesnay (Chapter I, note 13) terms these four lines "outrageous" and claims Ovid included them primarily to shock and amuse his audience (11). The amusement is accomplished specifically by the parody which creates humor.

jocular attitude towards the serious, troubled lover, a role played very effectively by Propertius in 2.23. Ovid mocks this particular Propertian stance in another type of parody also. In the *Amores* Ovid sometimes parodies a serious Propertian statement by using it in a mock heroic context. The flippant tone of the Ovidian imitation when contrasted with the melancholy associations of the Propertian original creates parody with its attendant humor.

This type of mock-heroic parody can be seen, for example, in *Am.* 1.13, Ovid's poetic *suasoria* to Aurora.[29]

Prop. 2.26B.29-30, 35-36:

seu mare per longum mea cogitet ire puella,
   hanc sequar et fidos una aget aura duos. ...
omnia perpetiar: saevus licet urgeat Eurus,
   velaque in incertum frigidus Auster agat;

Am. 1.13.25-26:

omnia perpeterer; sed surgere mane puellas
   quis, nisi cui non est ulla puella, ferat?[30]

Propertius in 2.26B is vowing his eternal love for Cynthia. The intensity of his passion, he claims, will be demonstrated by the severity of the hardships he will endure by her side. The Propertian role is the lover as hero, oblivious to danger as long as he can be next to his true love. When Ovid begins with the same words, one can only expect a similar heroic declaration. The introduction of a "danger" which can only be termed trivial effectively undercuts this expectation. That girls must arise from bed in the morning is scarcely an evil demanding heroic endurance. By introducing such a triviality, Ovid effectively parodies Propertian seriousness.[31]

Propertian endurance is parodied again in *Am.* 1.14.

---

[29] For a detailed analysis of the rhetorical aspects of this poem, see A. Elliott, "*Amores* 1.13: Ovid's Art" *CJ* 69 (1973-74) 127-32.

[30] Evidence for imitation here depends upon the verb *perpetior*. Augustan poets generally avoided this verb, perhaps because the *per*-intensive prefix was felt to be vulgar (see B. Axelson, *Unpoetische Wörter* [Lund, 1945] 37-8). *Patior* was much preferred. In Ovid, for example, *patior* is used over one hundred fifty times, *perpetior* only seven.

[31] The degree of seriousness of each elegist is also reflected in the mood of the verb. Propertius naturally chooses the indicative—his endurance is a fact. Ovid's subjunctive implies doubt about his ability to endure. This is one more way of lending this trivial "evil" an importance which it obviously does not deserve.

Prop. 1.1.25-28:

et vos, qui sero lapsum revocatis, amici,
    quaerite non sani pectoris auxilia.
fortiter et ferrum saevos patiemur et ignis,
    sit modo libertas quae velit ira loqui.

Am. 1.14.25-26:

quam se praebuerant, ferro patienter et igni,
    ut fieret torto nexilis orbe sinus.

In the first elegy of the Monobiblos, Propertius wants to convey the strength of the passion that has overwhelmed him. In his frantic search for a cure for his love, he confesses himself willing to undergo surgery. *Auxilia* is used here in its medicinal sense of "remedy." *Ferrum* refers to the knife of surgery, *ignes* to the cauterizing iron.[32] Ovid has adapted this surgical imagery to a new "patient." Instead of the heartsick lover who will endure medical treatment in an attempt to regain his sanity, Ovid gives us Corinna's hair. Treatment is needed to cure it of its straightness. The curling iron and the brazier to heat it become the specific surgical instruments needed for the operation. The terms *ferrum* and *ignis* thus take on a humorous double meaning. Also humorous is the fact that the "patient" has long since died! Additional humor, however, attends upon Ovid's general mockery of the Propertian stance of heroic endurance. The instruments which reflect the depths of Propertius' passion become simply amusing when applied to the locks of Corinna's hair.

In the next example, Ovid parodies Propertian seriousness of another kind.

Prop. 3.7.11-14:

sed tua nunc volucres astant super ossa marinae,
    nunc tibi pro tumulo Carpathium omne mare est.
infelix Aquilo, raptae timor Orithyiae,
    quae spolia ex illo tanta fuere tibi?

---

[32] *Cf.* Celsus 2.9, 2.11, 4.22 for *auxilia*; 7.3, 7.10 for *ferrum*: 5.27, 7.2 for *ignes*. See Enk (Chapter 1, note 5: *Liber Primus*, part 2) 16-17.

Am. 1.6. 51-54:

fallimur: impulsa est animoso ianua vento.

    ei mihi, quam longe spem tulit aura meam.

si satis es raptae, Borea, memor Orithyiae,

    huc ades et surdas flamine tunde foris.[33]

Prop. 3.7 is a very serious elegy, about the youth Paetus, who was lured to his death on the sea by his desire for wealth. Propertius' use of the name *Orithyia*, then, followed the general practice of Latin poets. The appearance of Orithyia was limited to serious mythological, usually epic, contexts.[34]

What is suitably serious in Propertius becomes parody in Ovid. He uses the Propertian reminiscence to introduce a humorous, mock-epic section of his paraclausithyron.[35] This would be humorous in and of itself since both Ovid's appeal to Boreas and his threats (57-58) are ridiculous in view of his situation. In addition, Ovid has rejected the stateliness of Propertius' mythological allusion in favor of the more prosaic art of persuasion. The myth of Boreas and Orithyia in his hands becomes a reason why the North Wind should break the door down for him. Ovid's insistence on the practical—the fact that Boreas having felt love himself should come to his aid—is what creates the parody and humor here.

If we consider the examples of parody discussed in this chapter, we can make several generalizations about Ovid as a parodist. Ovid's primary purpose in using parody was to create humor. In every case Ovid has turned serious verses of Propertius to a lighter vein. The elegies which include parody are generally written in a light, humorous manner to begin with.[36] They would be funny

---

[33] *Am.* 1.6.53 is one of the two spondaic hexameters in the *Amores*. (The other is *Am.* 2.13.21.) Propertius made proportionately more use of this device than Ovid did. M. Platnauer, *Latin Elegiac Verse* (Cambridge, 1951) 38-9 lists seven examples in Propertius' 2004 hexameters, 18 examples in Ovid's 11,010 elegiac hexameters. Ovid's usual restraint in using such lines may be additional evidence of Propertian influence here.

[34] The name is used by Verg. *G.* 4.463, *Aen.* 12.83; Prop. 1.20.31, 2.26.51, 3.7.13; Ov. *Am.* 1.6.53, *Met.* 6.683, 707, 7.695; Val. Fl. 1.468; Stat. *Th.* 12.630; Sil. 8.514, 12.526.

[35] Evidence of epic language is legion in *Am.* 1.6.53-58. In addition to the appearance of Orithyia, one might note the *-que -que* of line 57 (see Norden, *Vergilius Aen. VI*[4] [Stuttgart, 1957] 288), the joining of *ferro* with *igni* in a non-medical sense (*ThLL* 6.1.586. 7 ff.), and the use of *madeo* with *rore* (*ThLL* 8.33.64 ff.).

[36] Two possible exceptions are 1.6 and 2.9b. Even in 1.6, however, the specific passage where Ovid uses parody is a mock epic and is meant to be funny.

even without parody, but the inclusion of parody adds extra humor.

Moreover, Ovid prefers to avoid parody at the beginning of a poem. In his simpler, one or two line parodies Ovid places the imitation in the middle of his elegy, which is usually one of his longer narrative efforts.[37] The unobtrusiveness of the parody perhaps added to the fun of it. How many of Rome's *litterati* would recognize and enjoy these minor parodies?[38] The lengthier and more complicated parodies are given more prominent positions, as when Ovid parodies Propertius at the end of *Am.* 3.4 and 2.19. Obviously, then, Ovid planned his use of parody very carefully and achieved maximum effect by limited and selective use of the device. In every case when he does choose to parody, the humor of his elegy is enhanced.

---

[37] We have cited examples from *Am.* 1.2, 1.6, 1.13, 1.14, 2.5, 2.6, 2.9b, 2.19, 3.3, 3.4. With the exception of 2.9b (30 lines), the shortest of these poems is 48 lines (1.3, 3.3). The longest is 74 lines (1.6).

[38] So Frécaut (*supra*, note 3) speaks of "... une connivence entre l'écrivain qui place adroitement cette formule et le lecteur cultivé qui la découvre et s'en délecte" (114).

CHAPTER FOUR

OVID AS DAEDALUS: DIFFERENCE IN ATTITUDE

Many times in the *Amores* Ovid uses Propertian imitation to establish a specific background for his elegy. In one sense, of course, all imitation establishes background, since any successful imitation will bring to mind the lines or passage being imitated.[1] Often, however, the reminiscence is a fleeting one. This is particularly true for short imitations like most of those discussed in the chapter on parody. The imitation is included for a specific reason—in this case, the creation of humor—and is quickly forgotten once it has been recognized and appreciated. The background we shall be discussing in this chapter and the next is a much more complicated one. The imitations to be considered are not only longer but were included by Ovid for various, often complex reasons. They have in common, however, the bringing of a particular Propertian context to the Ovidian elegy.[2] The Propertian background thus created invariably enhances the meaning of Ovid's poem in important but usually subtle ways.[3] In the subtlety and complexity of these imitations, Ovid's artistry is clearly revealed.

One effect which Ovid often achieves through the use of Propertian background is contrast. Ovid in general adopts a light and playful tone in the *Amores*. Love is a game rather than a heart-rending passion. As a love elegist, Ovid is irreverent sometimes to the point of flippancy in his treatment of many of the conventional topics of the genre. While this attitude is easily apparent to any reader of the *Amores*, Ovid on occasion emphasizes it through direct contrast with Propertius. One way to accomplish this is through

---

[1] See A. Guillemin, "L'imitation dans les literatures antiques et en particulière dans la literature latine" *REL* 2 (1924) 35-57; E. Löfstedt, "Reminiscence and Imitation: Some Problems in Latin Literature" *Eranos* 47 (1949) 148-164.

[2] L. P. Wilkinson, "Greek Influence on the Poetry of Ovid" *Entretiens sur l'antiquité classique* (Fondation Hardt) Tome II (Vandoevres-Genève, 1956) 223-43, sees the imparting of a background as important in Ovid's use of Greek models. Ovid's use of it in regard to Catullus is touched upon by J. Ferguson, "Catullus and Ovid" *AJP* 80 (1960) 337-57.

[3] We have seen this general background operating once already, in *Am.* 3.1 (see Chapter II). When read with Prop. 3.3 in mind, Ovid's "message" about his future in elegy becomes clearer and more emphatic.

parody, as the last chapter has shown. There are, however, several elegies in the *Amores* where more complicated and subtle contrasts are developed. In each of these Ovid achieves ironic effects by establishing a particular Propertian background through direct imitation. The contrast between Ovid's poem and the Propertian context introduced in this fashion adds a new dimension to the Ovidian elegy.

Let us look first at *Am.* 1.3, an elegy usually interpreted as a serious Ovidian declaration of love for one girl, never named, who will be Ovid's only source of poetic inspiration. *Am.* 1.3 is meant to be read against the background of Prop. 3.2, an elegy which extols poetry's power to make any girl famous.

Ovid introduces Prop. 3.2 through a structural imitation.[4] (The pertinent words have been italicized.)

Prop. 3.2.11-16:

quod *non* Taenariis domus est mihi fulta columnis,
  nec camera auratas inter eburna trabes,
nec mea Phaeacas aequant pomaria silvas,
  non operosa rigat Marcius antra liquor;
at Musae comites et carmina cara legenti,
  et defessa choris Calliopea meis.

Am. 1.3.7-12:

si me *non* veterum commendant magna parentum
  nomina, *si* nostri sanguinis auctor eques,
nec meus innumeris renovatur campus aratris,
  temperat et sumptus parcus uterque parens:
at Phoebus comitesque novem vitis*que* repertor
  hac faciunt . . .

Both elegists are expressing the same idea: neither is rich but each possesses the power of poetry. *Am.* 1.3 develops with Ovid, both as a lover and a poet, vowing eternal fidelity to this one girl.

Am. 1.3.15-16:

non mihi mille placent, non sum desultor amoris:
  tu mihi, si qua fides, cura perennis eris.

---

[4] Neumann, 26-29, recognizes this imitation. He claims Ovid is very serious and is speaking of Corinna.

Am. 1.3.19-20:

te mihi materiem felicem in carmina praebe:
provenient causa carmina digna sua.

Am. 1.3.25-26:

nos quoque per totum pariter cantabimur orbem
iunctaque semper erunt nomina nostra tuis.

This is surely a strange attitude for Ovid, the playful lover, to display in his first poem that specifically mentions a girl.[5] Even stranger, if he is truly serious in his declarations, is the choice of Prop. 3.2 as a background poem for this elegy. Prop. 3.2 is hardly a Propertian avowal of passionate and eternal love for Cynthia. Rather, Propertius is rejoicing in the crowds of girls who are available to him because of his poetic ability.

Prop. 3.2.9-10:

miremur, nobis et Baccho et Apolline dextro,
turba puellarum si mea verba colit?

Prop. 3.2.17-18:

fortunata, meo si qua es celebrata libello!
carmina erunt formae tot monumenta tuae.

It is extremely likely, then, that Ovid is being ironic in *Am.* 1.3, not sincere.[6] At the same time that he is playing the role of the traditional lover-elegist by vowing total fidelity and devotion, he is subtly reminding the reader of the crowds of girls whose affections he could cultivate. It has been pointed out elsewhere that this irony is developed in part through Ovid's choice of mythological examples

---

[5] *Am.* 1.3 may be considered Ovid's third introductory poem. *Am.* 1.1 explains how Cupid forced Ovid into the genre of love elegy and *Am.* 1.2 gives a general picture of the poet in love, couched in terms of participation in Cupid's triumph. This, then, is the third poem about Ovid's creative processes, and in it both previous themes of writing love elegy and being in love coalesce and focus on the central figure of "the girl." The reader will, of course, immediately think of Cynthia or Lesbia, but Ovid's more subtle implications remain to be seen.

[6] L. C. Curran, "*Desultores amoris*: Ovid *Amores* 1.3" *CP* 61 (1966) 47-49, argues very convincingly on other grounds that Ovid is being ironic, not sincere. While he notes the imitation of Prop. 3.2.11-16, he fails to see its important implications for the irony of the poem. See also K. Olstein, "*Amores* 1.3 and Duplicity as a Way of Love" *TAPA* 105 (1975) 241-257.

(21-24).[7] In all of them, the poet is relegated to the role of Jove, the world's best known *desultor amoris*. The Propertian background makes the same point since once again Ovid shows how conscious he is of the other women waiting in the wings. Such ironic overtones make it difficult to accept Ovid's protestations at their face value. Read in this way, *Am.* 1.3 makes a fitting introduction to Ovid's general attitude towards love as we see it in the *Amores*.

In *Am.* 1.3 Ovid uses Propertian background to achieve an ironic effect. In *Am.* 3.12 Propertian imitation is instrumental in emphasizing Ovid's disillusionment with love elegy as a literary genre. Ordinarily, love elegists spoke of the genre in terms of the power it gave them in the pursuit of their beloved. Its usefulness was an important reason for their interest, or so they were fond of saying.[8] In *Am.* 3.12, however, Ovid reverses this usual attitude. Far from being an aid to him in winning Corinna's love, love elegy has proven a hindrance. His poems have made Corinna famous and have brought him rivals. In short, love elegy has harmful as well as beneficial power.

This is a theme which is very much in keeping with the general tone of the elegies at the end of the *Amores*.[9] However, Ovid also was aware of the novelty of his theme and indeed, emphasized it through contrast with Propertius. *Am.* 3.12 is meant to be read against the background of Prop. 2.8. Ovid introduces Prop. 2.8 early in his elegy.

Prop. 2.8.5-6;

possum ego in alterius positam spectare lacerto?
    nec mea dicetur, quae modo dicta mea est.

Am. 3.12.5-6:

quae modo dicta mea est, quam coepi solus amare,
    cum multis vereor ne sit habenda mihi.

---

[7] Curran, 48; Olstein, 244-6.
[8] *E.g.*, Prop. 1.7, 1.9, 2.34, 3.2; *Am.* 1.3, 2.1, 2.17, 3.1. In this last poem, Elegy herself explains her usefulness:

rustica sit sine me lascivi mater Amoris:
    huic ego proveni lena comesque deae.
                                        (3.1.43-44)
[9] This tone will be discussed in Chapter VI.

Propertius is also complaining about losing his girl, but in a much more general way. His girl is simply *eripitur* (2.8.1). No reason is given.

Propertius continues by discussing the vicissitudes of love in a very fatalistic way.

Prop. 2.8.7-12:

omnia vertuntur: certe vertuntur amores:
　vinceris aut vincis, haec in amore rota est.
magni saepe duces, magni cecidere tyranni,
　et Thebae steterant altaque Troia fuit.
munera quanta dedi vel qualia carmina feci!
　illa tamen numquam ferrea dixit 'Amo.'

Although Propertius mentions poetry, he does not specifically blame the effects of love elegy for the loss of his girl. In fact, he implies that poems were no more important in his suit than other types of gifts. He offers no answers in this particular poem, just accepts, however bitterly, the inevitable.[10]

Contrast Ovid's attitude in *Am.* 3.12 where he says about the loss of Corinna:

Am. 3.12.13-16:

an prosint dubium, nocuerunt carmina certe:
　invidiae nostris illa fuere bonis.
cum Thebae, cum Troia foret, cum Caesaris acta,
　ingenium movit sola Corinna meum.

Ovid is not fatalistic at all. In a line which surely echoes Propertius' *certe*,[11] Ovid states that he knows exactly where to place the blame —on his own poetry. For Propertius, the *carmina* were simply in-

---

[10] To some editors (Ribbeck, *e.g.*) the stoical quality of lines 7-10 has seemed so out of keeping with Propertian attitudes that they have assigned these four lines to Propertius' friend (addressed in line 2). H. E. Butler, *Sexti Properti Opera Omnia* (London, 1905) 185 would begin a new elegy at line 13. I am inclined to favor this solution for the problems inherent in Prop. 2.8 because Ovid in *Am.* 3.12 uses only Prop. 2.8.1-12 as his background material. For a defense of the poem's integrity, see Enk (Chapter 1, note 5: *Liber Secundus*, part 2) 119-20.

[11] One might also note the similarity between *Am.* 3.12.15 and Prop. 2.8.9-10. Caesar would thus become one of the *duces* or *tyranni* of Prop. 2.8.9. The latter is a bold equation on Ovid's part, but perhaps the subtlety of the allusion allowed it to escape general notice.

effectual gifts. For Ovid, they have become a destructive force. The effect, then, is one of contrast and irony—contrast because Ovid sees the dangers latent in love elegy while Propertius does not, irony because the thing which should have been helpful, or at the very least ineffectual, has been the source of all Ovid's troubles.

Even more extensive imitation of Propertius can be seen in *Am.* 2.4 and 2.10. Both of these poems, when read against their Propertian background, pointedly demonstrate the fundamental difference between the Propertian and the Ovidian lover. The seriousness of the one is contrasted with the frivolity of the other. *Am.* 2.4 and 2.10 are meant to be read against the background of Prop. 2.25 and 2.22A.[12] Since imitations of both Propertian elegies appear in each Ovidian poem, Prop. 2.25 and 2.22A may have been considered some sort of pair. In any event, Ovid clearly had both elegies in mind when he composed *Am.* 2.4 and 2.10. All four of these poems have as their subject the question of how many girls a man can and should love at one time. The two Propertian elegies are closely related to each other, not only in theme but also in tone. Propertius begins 2.22A:

> Scis here mi multas pariter placuisse puellas;
>   scis mihi, Demophoon, multa venire mala.
>
> > (Prop. 2.22A.1-2)

Prop. 2.25 begins on a different note:

> Unica nata meo pulcherrima cura dolori

but ends forty-eight lines later:

> cum satis una tuis insomnia portet ocellis,
>   una sat est cuivis femina multa mala.
>
> > (Prop. 2.25.47-48)

The tone in both poems is set by such words as *multa mala* and *dolor*. Love for Propertius, he would have us believe, is always a pain and a trial. It makes no difference whether he has one, two, or a dozen paramours.

It is this pessimistic Propertian attitude which Ovid contradicts

---

[12] Neumann, 63-68, notes the imitations of Prop. 2.22A and 2.25 in *Am.* 2.4 but claims that Prop. 2.22A is Ovid's major source. He does not emphasize the difference in tone. In *Am.* 2.10 he regards the primary influence as a letter of Aristaenetus (II.11) and Prop. 2.22A is a secondary influence (79-85) Again, he does not discuss the difference in tone.

in his own two elegies. Ovid's tone is, predictably, just the opposite
of his predecessor's. For example, he ends *Am.* 2.4 by stating:

Am. 2.4.47-48:

denique quas tota quisquam probat Urbe puellas,
    noster in has omnis ambitiosus amor.

Ovid does complain briefly in 2.10 about the problems of loving
two girls at once (11-12) but he promptly returns to his more
cheerful outlook on love, saying: [13]

Am. 2.10.15-16, 21-22:

sed tamen hoc melius, quam si sine amore iacerem:
    hostibus eveniat vita severa meis; ...
me mea disperdat nullo prohibente puella,
    si satis una potest, si minus una, duae.

Ovid establishes the Propertian background through an imitation
at the beginning of *Am.* 2.4:

Am. 2.4.1-10:

Non ego mendosos ausim defendere mores
    falsaque pro vitiis arma movere meis.
confiteor, si quid prodest delicta fateri;
    in mea nunc demens crimina fassus eo.
odi, nec possum cupiens non esse, quod odi:
    heu quam, quae studeas ponere, ferre grave est!
nam desunt vires ad me mihi iusque regendum;
    auferor, ut rapida concita puppis aqua.
non est certa meos quae forma invitet amores:
    centum sunt causae cur ego semper amem.

The second distich of this introduction is an imitation of Prop.
2.25.17-20: [14]

---

[13] I.M. Le M. DuQuesnay (Chapter I, note 13) sees in these lines the
main point for Ovid's imitation of Propertius in *Am.* 2.10. In Prop. 2.22A,
Propertius has advocated loving two women rather than one; Ovid compares
two women to none at all. Du Quesnay speaks of "the comic effect of this
sudden switch in direction" (21).

[14] I have not followed Barber's *OCT* at line 17. Using the conjectures
collected by W. R. Smyth, *Thesaurus Criticus ad Sexti Properti Textum,
Mnemosyne* suppl. 12 (1970) *ad loc.*, I have read *demens* (Palmer, 1874) for
dominae and *amator* (Heinsius, Müller, Ayrmann, Korsch) for *amor qui*.
The structural similarities (to be discussed next) and the common emphasis
on confession (*fateor, confiteor*) and motion (*eo, redit*) provide independent
evidence of imitation.

> at nullo demens teritur sub crimine amator:
>   restat et immerita sustinet aure minas.
> ultro contemptus rogat, et peccasse fatetur
>   laesus, et invitis ipse redit pedibus.

The parallelism continues in a structural vein, since Propertius' next distich ends ... *nulla diu femina pondus habet* (2.25.22). The idea of weight is echoed by Ovid in line 6. Propertius proceeds by introducing the image of a ship troubled by a storm:

Prop. 2.25.23-24:

> an quisquam in mediis persolvit vota procellis,
>   cum saepe in portu fracta carina natet?

This image is also used by Ovid (*Am.* 2.4.8).

A contrast of attitudes, then, is established by Ovid at the very beginning of *Am.* 2.4. The first ten lines of this elegy purport to be serious, but "the problem" to which Ovid obliquely alludes in his first four distichs is revealed to be his propensity for falling in love with every girl he sees. The Propertian lines, on the other hand, are truly serious. Propertius is discussing the very real problem (from the lover's point of view) of the fickleness of women in love. The passage which Ovid has been imitating thus concludes:

Prop. 2.25.27-28:

> mendaces ludunt flatus in amore secundi:
>   si qua venit sero, magna ruina venit.

Propertius' tone is bitter, Ovid's is light.

This contrast continues with Ovid's imitation of Prop. 2.25.39-42. By this point in his elegy Propertius has taken up the subject of loving many girls, although it is not the poet himself who is involved. Rather, he is speaking to certain unnamed people.

Prop. 2.25.39-42: [15]

> at, vos qui officia in multos revocatis amores,

---

[15] The text of Prop. 2.25.42 is often emended to read *fuscam* (Mueller, Enk, Barber's *OCT*) or *fuscas* (Markland) in order to allow the adjective to agree with *puellam* or *puellas*. I believe that on the basis of Ovid's imitation *fusco* should be retained. Propertius expected the reader to supply *colore* from his use of *color* at the end of the line. (Similarly Prop. 2.24b.35.) Ovid has made the slightly confusing Propertian expression totally straightforward and explicit.

> quantus sic cruciat lumina vestra dolor!
> vidistis pleno teneram candore puellam,
>   vidistis fusco, ducit uterque color.

The bitter tone is still in evidence as a few lines later Propertius tells us:

Prop. 2.25.46:

haec atque illa mali vulneris una via est.

Contrast this with Ovid's tone in his imitation:

Am. 2.4.39-40:

candida me capiet, capiet me flava puella;
  est etiam in fusco grata colore venus.

Propertius' *malum vulnus* has become Ovid's *grata venus*.

If we consider the contents of these two elegies, we must immediately notice the irony of Ovid's choice of model. *Am.* 2.4 is Ovid's "confession" that he cannot help loving all women, no matter what their physical and mental attributes. Yet one of the major themes of Prop. 2.25 is the fickleness of women. Has Ovid set up this Propertian background—the fickleness of woman theme —to vindicate himself for his own fickle conduct? If we accept this idea, the first distich of Ovid's poem takes on new meaning. Ovid may not be defending his way of life directly, with words, but he certainly is making an indirect defense by reminding the reader through Propertian imitation that women, too, are fickle. Changing partners is simply part of the game of love.

One further Propertian imitation, from Prop. 2.22A rather than Prop. 2.25, supports this point of view.

Prop. 2.22A.17-18:

uni cuique dedit vitium natura creato:
  mi fortuna aliquid semper amare dedit.

Am. 2.4.9-10:

non est certa meos quae forma invitet amores:
  centum sunt causae cur ego semper amem.

The strong Propertian echo ... *semper amem* adds both to the irony of *Am.* 2.4 and to Ovid's defense of himself.[16] In 2.22A Propertius,

---

[16] This imitation is noted by many editors, including Brandt (Chapter I, note 5) 97. Neumann, 64, explicitly mentions it in his discussion of *Am.* 2.4.

like Ovid in *Am.* 2.4, admits to loving many girls at once. He seems most distressed at the prospect saying that it brings him *multa mala* (line 2) and even calling his propensity for falling in love a *vitium*, a word echoed by Ovid at *Am.* 2.4.2. This Propertian imitation follows directly upon the imitation of Prop. 2.25.17-20 discussed above. If with that imitation Ovid is defending himself by subtly reminding the reader that women are fickle too, with this imitation his defense becomes even more clever. For Propertius as we saw him in 2.25 was a zealous advocate of confining oneself to one love. He also inveighed fiercely against the fickleness of women. Now, at *Am.* 2.4.9-10, Ovid shows us Propertius confessing his own fickleness. If even such a strong proponent of the "one-girl-at-a-time" theory can be overcome by *vitium*, how can we blame Ovid for his *mendosos mores* (1)? The juxtaposition of imitations thus provides Ovid's defense.

Ovid makes use of the same two Propertian models and the same basic themes in *Am.* 2.10. *Am.* 2.10, however, is more closely connected to Prop. 2.22A than it is to Prop. 2.25. The structure of Ovid's elegy is virtually identical to that of Prop. 2.22A. Both poets address their elegies to friends whose names appear in the first distich. The two poems are organized as follows: 1) a ten line introduction which states the problem; 2) four lines of questions in which the poet asks why he has the problem; [17] 3) an answer justifying his behavior (four lines in Prop. 2.22A, eight lines in *Am.* 2.10); 4) a short expression of confidence in the poet's own sexual potency, which is made more emphatic in Prop. 2.22A through the use of mythological examples; 5) a wish which concludes each elegy. The only real structural difference between *Am.* 2.10 and Prop. 2.22A is the lack of mythological examples in Ovid's elegy.[18]

In addition to the clear structural similarity, *Am.* 2.10 contains some explicit imitations of Prop. 2.22A and 2.25.

Am. 2.10.11-12:

quid geminas, Erycina, meos sine fine dolores?
    non erat in curas una puella satis?

---

[17] I am omitting Prop. 2.22A.11-12, following Housman and Barber. For other possible solutions to the problem posed by these lines, see W. R. Smyth (*supra*, note 14) *ad loc.* The structural parallelism with *Am.* 2.10 provides additional evidence for excising these lines.

[18] I. M. Le M. Du Quesnay (Chapter I, note 13) 21-22 claims that Ovid has deliberately omitted mythology and inserted an example drawn from his own experience, thus heightening his "bold impudence" by suggesting "that he is to be compared with Achilles or Hector."

Am. 2.10.11 is surely meant to recall the last line of Prop. 2.22A:

tutius et geminos anxia mater alit (42),

while the second line of this distich is reminiscent of the last line
of Prop. 2.25:

una sat est cuivis femina multa mala (48).

These imitations have an important position in *Am.* 2.10 because
they follow directly upon the ten-line introduction. In the course
of this introduction Ovid has stated his problem—he is in love with
two girls at once—in very gloomy terms. The pessimistic mood is
reinforced by these two imitations, since the end of both Propertian
elegies speaks of love for more than one girl as a negative thing.[19]

It is important that Ovid establish the general pessimistic mood
of Prop. 2.22A and Prop. 2.25 so that his break with Propertius,
his assertion of his own completely positive attitude towards
women, will make a greater impression. The structural parallelism
which continues throughout the poem is one means to this end.
Ovid's affirmation of faith in his sexual powers, couched in words
reminiscent of Prop. 2.22A, is another.

Prop. 2.22A.21-24:

sed tibi si exilis videor tenuatus in artus,
    falleris: haud umquam est culta labore Venus.
percontere licet: saepe est experta puella
    officium tota nocte valere meum.

Am. 2.10.23-28:

sufficiam: graciles, non sunt sine viribus artus;
    pondere, non nervis, corpora nostra carent.
et lateri dabit in vires alimenta voluptas:
    decepta est opera nulla puella mea;
saepe ego lascive consumpsi tempora noctis,
    utilis et forti corpore mane fui.

---

[19]. Even though Propertius eventually does decide in 2.22A that two
girls are better than one, he does it for negative reasons—he is afraid of
rejection.

altera me cupidis teneat foveatque lacertis,
    altera si quando non sinit esse locum.
                                    (2.22A.37-38)

At this point, Ovid departs drastically from the tone of his Propertian models. Propertius in 2.22A proceeds to a consideration of loving two girls at once, the subject from which *Am.* 2.10 started. Propertius agrees that this may indeed be the best plan for the lover, but practical considerations rather than sensuality lead him to that conclusion. After Ovid's expression of confidence in his sexual powers, then, the reader who is aware of the Propertian background expects a return to Ovid's original theme and a grudging acceptance of the condition of loving two women at once. Instead, Ovid bursts out:

Am. 2.10.29-30; 35-38:

felix, quem Veneris certamina mutua perdunt;
    di faciant, leti causa sit ista mei! ...
at mihi contingat Veneris languescere motu,
    cum moriar, medium solvar et inter opus;
atque aliquis nostro lacrimans in funere dicat
    'conveniens vitae mors fuit ista tuae.'

Am. 2.10 ends on a note of unrestrained happiness about the joys of sex. We are no longer concerned with the question of one girl, two girls, or many girls, just the poet's ardent desire to be sexual and, in fact, to die in the midst of the sex act.[20] The impact of Ovid's affirmation of total sensuality is increased because of its contrast with the practical but decidedly less sexual recommendations of Propertius in 2.22A and 2.25.

Another difference in attitude between Ovid and Propertius becomes apparent in elegies which purport to treat the theme of traditional morality. Propertius is often the defender of traditional moral standards. Ovid, as we might expect, tends to adopt an amoral, or even an immoral stance.[21] This attitude is noticeable

---

[20] This passage also shows in a more general way a difference of attitude between Propertius and Ovid. Propertius is very concerned with his own death and funeral, particularly in regard to Cynthia's feelings and reactions to it (see, *e.g.,* Prop. 1.17.15-24, 2.13B). Ovid has moved from death, the final proof of eternal devotion, to death, the final proof of total sensuality. *Cf.* D. Donnet, "Ovide, Properce et l'élégie latine" *LEC* 33 (1965) 253-79, particularly 261, for a similar view.

[21] A good example of this can be seen in the treatment each poet gives to women of old-fashioned virtue. These passages are found in Prop. 2.25 and

many times in the *Amores*, but twice Ovid emphasizes it through direct imitation of Propertius. The shorter of these imitations is found in *Am*. 1.6, Ovid's paraclausithyron.[22]

The poem of the door and the locked-out lover had already been established as a traditional theme of Latin elegy.[23] Both Catullus and Propertius had preceded Ovid in writing paraclausithyra, but Ovid's poem differs from theirs in some important ways. The earlier elegists present the door itself speaking. In Catullus 67, a dialogue is carried on between the poet and the door. In Prop. 1.16, the door delivers a monologue which includes, however, a lament by an unnamed, locked-out lover. Ovid has personalized the poem. *Am*. 1.6 consists of a long speech made by the poet outside the door, addressing himself not to the door itself, but to the *ianitor*. This device, of course, increases the suspense since the *ianitor*, unlike the *ianua*, is capable of action. In addition, both Catullus' and Propertius' elegies have a strong moralistic tinge. The behavior of the woman of the house is in each case lamented by the door which serves her. *Am*. 1.6 offers no such judgments.

Ovid's speech in *Am*. 1.6 consists of a series of pleas separated by a refrain which divides the poem into five stanzas. At line 19, Ovid emphasizes the doorkeeper's humanity (and his lowly status) by reminding him of past favors.

Am. 2.4, so it is possible that Ovid meant to establish a direct comparison. Philological evidence, however, is lacking.

Prop. 2.25.35-36:
at si saecla forent antiquis grata puellis,
    essem ego quod nunc tu: tempore vincor ego.

Am. 2.4.15-16:
aspera si visa est rigidasque imitata Sabinas,
    velle sed ex alto dissimulare puto.

Propertius takes virtue seriously; Ovid shrugs it off as a pretense.

[22] *Am*. 1.6 is unique in containing four unrelated imitations of Propertius. Two of these (1.6.9-14, 53-54) have been discussed in Chapter III. *Am*. 1.6.49-52 will be treated in Chapter V. Since is is slightly disconcerting to have so many different, unrelated Propertian references, perhaps *Am*. 1.6 was something of an experiment on Ovid's part. It is also the only poem in the *Amores* where Ovid uses a refrain.

[23] For the history of the paraclausithyron, see F. Copley, *Exclusus Amator, Phil. Monographs of the APA* 17 (1956), 1-42. For his rather negative view of Ovid's paraclausithyron, see 125-40.

Am. 1.6.19-20:

certe ego, cum posita stares ad verbera veste,
    ad dominam pro te verba tremente tuli.

The theme is continued immediately following the refrain (24) when
Ovid wishes that the slave might achieve his freedom.

Am. 1.6.25-26:

excute: sic umquam longa relevere catena,
    nec tibi perpetuo serva bibatur aqua.

A hidden meaning lurks here, however, since Ovid has based his
verse on Propertius.

Prop. 1.9.1-3:

Dicebam tibi venturos, irrisor, amores,
    nec tibi perpetuo libera verba fore.
ecce iaces supplexque venis ad iura puellae.

When viewed in the light of the beginning of Prop. 1.9, Ovid can
only be threatening the *ianitor* with a place on the other side of the
door. A full dose of love's miseries may easily be awaiting him. The
implication is that he should be more sympathetic to the suffering
suppliant, namely Ovid, who is begging admittance.

This theme of the doorman's humanity culminates at lines 45-46
of the poem.

forsitan et tecum tua nunc requiescit amica:
    heu, melior quanto sors tua sorte mea.

Ovid has included this as another appeal for sympathy from his
adversary. However, the contrast between the stern, moralistic
doors of Cat. 67 and Prop. 1.16 and Ovid's easily corruptible *ianitor*
could hardly be more clearly presented. Not only is the man human
and likely to fall in love, Ovid now states that the *ianitor* may at
that very moment be preoccupied with sex. Such a doorkeeper can
be no judge of morals. He would never say, as Propertius' door does:

Prop. 1.16.47-48:

sic ego nunc dominae vitiis et semper amantis
    fletibus aeterna differor invidia.

Ovid accomplishes a similar contrast of attitude in his *lena* poem. *Am.* 1.8 is based almost entirely on Prop. 4.5 and constitutes Ovid's closest and most extensive imitation of his predecessor.[24] There is a major difference, however. Ovid's poem is clearly designed to emphasize the general amorality of Roman society. The numerous imitations of Propertius are directed towards one end, contrasting the Propertian world view in which moral distinctions are still valid with this basically amoral world view of Ovid. Prop. 4.5 retains a tone of moral indignation. Ovid in *Am.* 1.8 is much more resigned and accepting of the *lena*'s "outrageous" conduct.

That *Am.* 1.8 is an imitation of Prop. 4.5 is evident from the structural similarity of the two poems. Each elegy has as its core a long speech given by an old *lena* to a young, pretty girl.[25] Before the speech, at the beginning of each elegy, the *lena* is presented in a four-line introduction and her powers as a witch are then described.[26] Finally, following the *lena*'s speech, each elegist adds a conclusion in which he displays his personal feelings about the old woman.[27] Although there are differences in the number of lines assigned to these various sections, the basic structure of the two poems is remarkably similar.

The character of the *lena* is revealed in part through the use of narrative at the beginning and end of each poem. In the Propertian narrative, two points are emphasized. The *lena* is a truly fearsome creature and the poet feels tremendous hatred towards her. This hatred is most clearly expressed through the curses that begin and end Prop. 4.5. Propertius opens his elegy with the wish that the *lena* may, like Tantalus, suffer thirst in the Underworld.

---

[24] Concerning Ovid's dependence on Prop. 4.5 in *Am.* 1.8, see Neumann, 106-22; Tränkle (Chapter I, note 15) 106 ff.; O. Kratins, "The Pretended Witch: A Reading of Ovid's *Amores* 1.8" *PhQ* 42 (1963) 151-58; R. Reitzenstein, *Hellenistische Wundererzählungen*[2] (Stuttgart, 1963) 155; G. Williams (Chapter I, note 17) 243-46.

[25] The speech of the *lena* in *Am.* 1.8 is by far the longer, running to eighty-six lines. The Propertian *lena* speaks only forty lines if one accepts Prop. 4.5.55-56 as an interpolation. For arguments about this, see U. Knoche, "Zur Frage der Properzinterpolation" *RhM* 85 (1936) 8-63, 16-20 for the lines in question. The majority of editors agree with Knoche that these lines do not really belong in Prop. 4.5 (see W. R. Smyth [*supra*, note 14]).

[26] Ovid's description of his *lena*'s powers is eighteen lines long. The Propertian description probably occupies sixteen lines. However, the last two lines (19-20) are hopelessly corrupt and some editors have made them the beginning of the *lena*'s speech (see W. R. Smyth [*supra*, note 14]).

[27] Ovid's conclusion is only six lines long; Propertius' is fourteen lines.

Prop. 4.5.1-4:

Terra tuum spinis obducat, lena, sepulcrum,
    et tua, quod non vis, sentiat umbra sitim;
nec sedeant cineri Manes, et Cerberus ultor
    turpia ieiuno terreat ossa sono!

The grave, thirst, and lack of peace for the dead reappear in the
curse at the end of 4.5.

Prop. 4.5.75-78:

sit tumulus lenae curto vetus amphora collo:
    urgeat hunc supra vis, caprifice, tua.
quisquis amas, scabris hoc bustum caedite saxis,
        mixtaque cum saxis addite verba mala.

Propertius also shows his loathing of the old woman by his joyous
reaction when he realizes how sickly and how near to death she is.
He promises an offering to Venus:

Prop. 4.5.65-66:

sed (cape torquatae, Venus o regina, columbae
    ob meritum ante tuos guttura secta focos).

Propertius' hatred for the *lena* has its counterpart in her open
hostility towards him. Propertius tells the reader not only about
the old woman's general powers of witchcraft, but about the designs
and charms she has used against him personally.

Prop. 4.5.17-18:

consuluitque striges nostro de sanguine, et in me
    hippomanes fetae semina legit equae.

In addition, the *lena* is poisoning the mind of Propertius' own girl
friend (63) and the poet has had previous altercations with the old
woman, or at least with her dog (73).

Propertius increases his *lena*'s fearsome qualities by his description of her as a completely immoral individual. The most sacred
institutions of Roman society—the home and family—are attacked
by her. Throughout the fourteen-line description of the *lena*'s
powers as a witch, the emphasis is on her destruction of moral and
noble instincts as they relate to sex and the family structure.

Prop. 4.5.5-8:

docta vel Hippolytum Veneri mollire negantem,
    concordique toro pessima semper avis,
Penelopen quoque neglecto rumore mariti
    nubere lascivo cogeret Antinoo.

After describing the witch's power to destroy the chastity of
Hippolytus and the faithfulness of Penelope, Propertius broadens
her sphere of action. She also will attack all watchful, i.e., old-
fashioned, moral husbands, causing them to suffer the fate of
blindness.

Prop. 4.5.15-16:

posset ut intentos astu caecare maritos,
    cornicum immeritas eruit ungue genas.

Even the *lena*'s power over nature is described in these terms:

Prop. 4.5.9-10:

illa velit, poterit magnes non ducere ferrum,
    et volucris nidis esse noverca suis.

The *lena* impinges not only on chastity and the marriage vow, but
on motherhood as well. She is terrifying because of her vicious acts
and also because of her immoral and anti-social attempts to destroy
the fabric of the family.[28]

Ovid's mood is much gentler and less angry than his predecessor's.
Instead of beginning his elegy with a curse, Ovid introduces his
lena in the following manner:

Am. 1.8.1-4:

Est quaedam (quicumque volet cognoscere lenam,
    audiat), est quaedam nomine Dipsas anus.
ex re nomen habet: nigri non illa parentem
    Memnonis in roseis sobria vidit equis.

The name Dipsas is a direct borrowing from Prop. 4.5.2. However,
Ovid from the very beginning deemphasizes the horror of his *lena*

---

[28] Although he is not, of course, officially married to the girl, Propertius
has taken upon himself the role of husband. This is apparent from his use of
the possessive *nostra* in reference to his girl friend (63). Also, he places the
description of the *lena*'s attempts against him directly following the line
about her attack on the *intentos maritos* (15).

and decreases the elements of personal involvement and anger. So
in these first four lines, Ovid proceeds to explain that the *lena* was
named Dipsas because she is a drunk. With the introduction of an
alcoholic *lena*, horror changes to humor.

Ovid's conclusion, too, shows dependence on Prop. 4.5 but again,
as in the first four lines, the tone is much less bitter. *Am.* 1.8 ends
with the following six lines:

Am. 1.8.109-114:

vox erat in cursu, cum me mea prodidit umbra;
    at nostrae vix se continuere manus
quin albam raramque comam lacrimosaque vino
    lumina rugosas distraherentque genas.
di tibi dent nullosque lares inopemque senectam
    et longas hiemes perpetuamque sitim.

Almost all of these elements are found in Propertius' conclusion.
Raramque comam corresponds to *rari...capilli* (Prop. 4.5.71) and
rugosas...genas are reminiscent of Propertius' *rugoso...collo*
(4.5.67). The *lacrimosa vino lumina* is Ovid's own invention, and
again, is designed to decrease the fearsome quality of the *lena* by
emphasizing that she is only an old drunk. Ovid's *nullos lares,
inopem senectam*, and *longas hiemes* reflect the ideas of extreme
poverty and cold expressed in Prop. 4.5.69-70. *Perpetuam sitim*,
the note on which Ovid ends, reflects the *amphora* of Prop. 4.5.75,
and once again emphasizes the drinking habits of the old woman.

The two conclusions are thus composed of the same elements, yet
the tones are entirely different. Propertius actually describes the
horrible, squalid death of his *lena* and ends with a second bitter
curse. Ovid's *lena* suffers no penalty at all. The poet claims he is
tempted to attack her, but he doesn't. Moreover, the curse he
invokes in his last two lines is extremely mild when compared with
the ending of Prop. 4.5. Propertius' involvement is total even to
the point of rejoicing at the old woman's death. Ovid's is peripheral.
He becomes momentarily angry, but only to the point of uttering
a mild curse.

The tone of lesser involvement is continued throughout Ovid's
description of his *lena*'s powers. Much of this section also is direct
imitation of Prop. 4.5.

Am. 1.8.7-8:

scit bene quid gramen, quid torto concita rhombo
  licia, quid valeat virus amantis equae.

Propertius' distich about *hippomanes* (4.5.17-18) describes the *lena* using it specifically against him. Ovid is much more general.[29]

Am 1.8.11-15:

sanguine, si qua fides, stillantia sidera vidi;
  purpureus Lunae sanguine vultus erat.
hanc ego nocturnas versam volitare per umbras
  suspicor et pluma corpus anile tegi;
suspicor, et fama est; ...

These lines correspond to Prop. 4.5.13-16, where the Propertian *lena* is described as charming the moon, changing herself into a wolf and attacking crows. Ovid has the *lena* turn into a bird, not a wolf. He further decreases the sense of horror by reminding us that it is a *corpus anile* that is being covered by feathers. And just in case any vestige of fear might remain, he takes pains to assure us that he doesn't even know if the story is true. Within these five lines, we find two uses of *suspicor*, a *si qua fides*, and a *fama est*.[30] Propertius, on the other hand, presented all of his *lena*'s actions as true and unassailable facts. Furthermore, Ovid's double use of *sanguine* here may be meant to recall the one use of *sanguine* in the introduction to Prop. 4.5. There the *lena* is seeking Propertius' own blood (line 17). Here, however, Ovid has removed the idea of blood far away from himself. The moon and stars may be associated with blood in this poem, but the poet himself is not.

The Ovidian pose of lesser anger and lesser involvement contributes greatly to the mood Ovid is establishing in *Am.* 1.8. Propertius is angry because the *lena* is harming him and his rela-

---

[29] Tränkle (Chapter I, note 15) 107 points out that Propertius' use of the word *hippomanes* itself rather than a euphemism (*cf.* Ovid's *virus amantis equae*) contributes to the harsh and angry tone of the Propertian poem.
[30] G. Williams (Chapter I, note 17) 546 makes this point, that Ovid describes the *lena*'s powers ironically, keeping in mind that the reader may not believe him. He also claims, however, that Ovid meant the reader to think of Corinna because of the placement of the poem. It is difficult to believe that the specific girl in question was important.

tionship by her immoral advice. Ovid does not appear convinced that the old woman is really harmful. This becomes clear from *Am.* 1.8.19-20:

> haec sibi proposuit thalamos temerare pudicos;
>   nec tamen eloquio lingua nocente caret.

While Propertius emphasized his *lena*'s powers to destroy sexual morality and the family structure, this distich is Ovid's only reference to such things. He limits his *lena*'s potential influence to *thalamos . . . pudicos*. Herein lies the irony of the situation, for Ovid proceeds to have his *lena* expound upon modern morals. In the process (23-48) she convinces us that there is no such thing as a "chaste marriage chamber" in modern day Rome. She herself is rendered harmless since her powers apply only to the chaste. The elegy can thus be viewed as an amusing joke. Ovid pretends to be annoyed with an old, drunk woman who can do no harm anyway, because old fashioned morality in regard to love, sex and marriage has long since disappeared.

Clearly Ovid meant to create a contrast between the moral climate as viewed by him and as viewed by Propertius. To this end he has carefully modelled the beginning of his *lena*'s speech to express direct opposition to much of what we find in Prop. 4.5. The Propertian *lena* never directly expounds on the situation at Rome. She begins her speech by flaunting six symbols of luxury before the girl in rapid succession. The abruptness of this beginning is continued in the series of short commands which make up the next two lines:

> Prop. 4.5.21-28:
>
> Si te Eoa Dorozantum iuvat aurea ripa,
>   et quae sub Tyria concha superbit aqua,
> Eurypylique placet Coae textura Minervae,
>   sectaque ab Attalicis putria signa toris,
> seu quae palmiferae mittunt venalia Thebae,
>   murreaque in Parthis pocula cocta focis;
> sperne fidem, provolve deos, mendacia vincant,
>   frange et damnosae iura pudicitiae!

The position of these commands is significant. The *lena* must be aware of the common rules of morality since she does not dare to give her shocking orders until she has made the girl receptive by listing symbols of wealth. These ideas only become palatable when tied to the girl's greed. This is clearly implied when the old woman says, *frange . . . iura pudicitiae* (28). If the girl is to "break the law," she is going to become the maverick, the social misfit. Other people, or at least the great majority of them, we must believe, were abiding by this "law of chastity." Following these eight lines, the Propertian *lena* begins giving specific advice to the girl on how to make money.

Ovid, by diverging at this point from the Propertian structure, emphasizes the different way in which his *lena* opens her speech. Twenty-six lines later (49) Ovid reverts to close imitation of Propertius when his *lena* too gives specific advice on how to make money. Meanwhile, though, the *lena* begins her speech by making immoral suggestions to the girl (23-34). The girl's reaction is quick and old fashioned—*erubuit* (35). It is the *lena's* response to this vestige of traditional morality that is most revealing about the moral climate of the times. The old woman can respond to the blush of embarrassment only in the most cynical of ways:

Am. 1.8.35-36:

erubuit! decet alba quidem pudor ora, sed iste,
   si simules, prodest; verus obesse solet.

The *lena* then discusses general conditions at Rome:

Am. 1.8.39-44:

forsitan immundae Tatio regnante Sabinae
   noluerint habiles pluribus esse viris;
nunc Mars externis animos exercet in armis,
   at Venus Aeneae regnat in urbe sui.
ludunt formosae: casta est quam nemo rogavit;
   aut, si rusticitas non vetat, ipsa rogat.

Her statements imply social conditions very different from those operating in Prop. 4.5. The girl in *Am.* 1.8 is a maverick and social misfit if she *doesn't* play the game of love. Society now expects this type of behavior. This difference in social conditions is reinforced by the contrast between *Am.* 1.8.43-44 and the advice given by Propertius' *lena* at 4.5.41-42:

nec te Medeae delectent probra sequacis
   (nempe tulit fastus ausa rogare prior).

Ovid has directly contradicted his predecessor. In the Propertian elegy, advances made by the woman could only bring her trouble. In *Am.* 1.8 this forwardness is presented as acceptable social behavior. In fact, it is almost mandatory for sophisticated Roman women, since all who avoid it are consigned to the dreary realm of *rusticitas*.

Another clear indication of the different moral climates of these two elegies is found in the first line of the speech of Ovid's *lena*. In this very emphatic position Ovid includes the only Propertian imitation not taken from 4.5. He imitates instead the first line of Prop. 2.22A.

Prop. 2.22A.1-2:

Scis here mi multas pariter placuisse puellas;
    scis mihi, Demophoon, multa venire mala.

Am. 1.8.23-24:

'scis here te, mea lux, iuveni placuisse beato?
    haesit et in voltu constitit usque tuo.'

In Prop. 2.22A the poet discusses how he is unable to keep from falling in love. In fact, he says, every girl has some attribute which captures him. Propertius mentions his sexual prowess (21-24) and concludes by saying that at any given time it is better to be in love with two girls than with one (35-42). This is hardly a poem in which Propertius advocates a monogamous relationship. Ovid's use of this elegy thus adds to his picture of general immorality at Rome. Even Propertius, Ovid's morally outraged predecessor, is in the final analysis no paragon of virtue. This imitation, then, provides the final and most concrete proof of Ovid's desire to render his *lena* harmless. *She* is not destroying morality. That has long since disappeared from Roman society, and the Ovidian *lena* is simply telling the girl how things are in modern Rome.

Once Ovid has established the feeling of a different, more sophisticated moral climate, he returns to close imitation of Propertius. Most of the specific pieces of advice delivered by his *lena* can be found in the earlier elegy.[31] Since the advice passages are in general so

---

[31] Two examples will suffice to show the similarity.

Prop. 4.5.35-6:

ingerat Aprilis Iole tibi, tundat Amyclc
    natalem Mais Idibus esse tuum.

similar, it is interesting to note the differences in what is said by the two *lenae*. The only advice which Ovid does not take from Propertius has to do with "modern" female behavior. Thus, when Ovid's *lena says*:

Am. 1.8.67-68:

> quin, quia pulcher erit, poscet sine munere noctem;
>   quod det, amatorem flagitet ante suum,

we realize that in Ovid's Rome, women are just as susceptible as men to the charms of a beautiful member of the opposite sex. Only her devotion to making money will keep the girl from going to bed for the pure enjoyment of it. There is also one piece of Propertian advice which Ovid ignores.

Prop. 4.5.45-46:

> in mores te verte viri: si cantica iactat,
>   i comes et voces ebria iunge tuas.

Male dominance, one of the basic tenets of traditional Roman marriage, is not formally acknowledged in the more sophisticated, less traditionally moral atmosphere of *Am.* 1.8.

Ovid's use of Propertian imitation to create a background against which all or part of his own elegy should be read constitutes the most extensive and complicated type of imitation in the *Amores*. So far, we have examined poems in which Ovid used Propertian background to emphasize differences in particular views and attitudes. Ovid's use of Propertius was in no way haphazard. Imitations of the older elegist were introduced to enhance the irony of a situation or to create an important contrast. There are no hard and fast rules about how, when or why Ovid used such imitations.

Am. 1.8.93-4:
cum te deficient poscendi munera causae,
  natalem libo testificare tuum.

Prop. 4.5.39-40:
semper habe morsus circa tua colla recentis,
  litibus alternis quos putet esse datos.

Am. 1.8.97-8:
ille viri videat toto vestigia lecto
  factaque lascivis livida colla notis.

We should perhaps be content to note that he always imitated creatively.

A particularly good example of this is *Am.* 1.8. In this, the most extensive Propertian imitation in the *Amores*, Propertius has provided Ovid with both his basic structure and ideas. If, however, we look beneath the surface similarities, it becomes apparent that Ovid took as much as he did from Prop. 4.5 in order to emphasize his own tone and point of view. The poem is totally Ovidian although it has been constructed on a Propertian base. Such creative imitation is the norm rather than the exception, as the examples in this chapter clearly demonstrate.

CHAPTER FIVE

OVID AS DAEDALUS: CHANGE OF MOOD

Lengthy and subtle imitation in the *Amores* is by no means limited to elegies in which Ovid expresses attitudes differing from those of his predecessors. Complex imitation is also common when Ovid is about to initiate a change of mood. Sometimes this change of mood occurs at an actual break in the poem, i.e. at the division between the two parts of a poetic pair. At other times the change of mood is part of the ongoing structure of a single poem.

Ovid uses imitation in two distinct ways when he is about to change the mood of a poem. First, he may set up a Propertian background which will effectively strengthen the contrast of moods. Generally this involves surprising the reader. Ovid's choice of imitation leads us to expect one thing and then something else actually happens. Second, Ovid may use imitation to provide clues about the impending change.[1] These hints are always subtle and depend for their success on the association of the Propertian context with what is about to happen in the Ovidian elegy. While such imitations do not change the basic meaning of the elegy, they allow the erudite reader to pride himself on anticipating the change of mood.

The simplest of these imitations is found in *Am.* 1.6, Ovid's paraclausithyron.[2] Ovid uses Propertius in this instance to generate a minor amount of suspense, closely followed by surprise. Things do not develop for Ovid as we would expect given the context of the Propertian imitation.

Prop. 4.8.49-52:

cum subito rauci sonuerunt cardine postes,
  et levia ad primos murmura facta Laris.
nec mora, cum totas resupinat Cynthia valvas,
  non operosa comis, sed furibunda decens.

---

[1] This device has been noticed by others. For instance, in regard to the *Metamorphoses* H. Fränkel says: "Ovid, a singularly considerate man, saw to it that the sudden change in his intentions should not come as a shock to his readers. He did not belong to that class of authors who are bent on doing justice to their subject only and forget their audience." (*Ovid: A Poet Between Two Worlds* [Berkeley, 1945] 102). J. Ferguson (Chapter I, note 2) discusses *Met.* 3.353-355 (an imitation of Cat. 62.42-44) in terms of this device.

[2] For other imitations in Ovid's paraclausithyron, see Chapter III, pages 36-37; Chapter IV, pages 56-58.

Am. 1.6.49-52:

fallimur, an verso sonuerunt cardine postes
    raucaque concussae signa dedere fores?
fallimur: inpulsa est animoso ianua vento.
    ei mihi, quam longe spem tulit aura meam!

Ovid is still, at *Am.* 1.6.49, waiting outside the door in the hopes
that the doorman will finally decide to admit him. He has a brief
glimmer of hope, only to realize two lines later that he has been
deceived. In Prop. 4.8, the poet was not deceived. He actually did
hear the sound of the hinges moving and the doors actually did
open to reveal Cynthia. Ovid's use of this Propertian imitation,
then, primes the reader to expect action. Something ought to happen.
This makes the frustration and disappointment of lines 51 and 52
even more intense. Instead of the doors being flung open to reveal
a beautiful if angry girl, we are told that the noise was caused by
nothing more than the wind. In a nice ironic touch, Ovid describes
his wind as *animosus*, a milder counterpart to Propertius' description of Cynthia as *furibunda*.

At the beginning of *Am.* 1.10, we find a more complicated example
of imitation used to elicit surprise. A seven-line passage which is
structurally parallel to Prop. 1.3.1-8 is used by Ovid to introduce a
Propertian background.

Prop. 1.3.1-8:

Qualis Thesea iacuit cedente carina
    languida desertis Cnosia litoribus;
qualis et accubuit primo Cepheia somno
    libera iam duris cotibus Andromede;
nec minus assiduis Edonis fessa choreis
    qualis in herboso concidit Apidano:
talis visa mihi mollem spirare quietem
    Cynthia ...

Am. 1.10.1-7:

Qualis ab Eurota Phrygiis avecta carinis
    coniugibus belli causa duobus erat,
qualis erat Lede, quam plumis abditus albis
    callidus in falsa lusit adulter ave,
qualis Amymone siccis erravit in Argis,
    cum premeret summi verticis urna comas,
talis eras ...

This Propertian simile comparing Cynthia to three sleeping mytho-logical figures creates a mood of romantic idealization.[3] The sleeping Cynthia is a beautiful sight. Ovid has indirectly transferred this mood to the beginning of his own elegy through the use of a simile reminiscent of Prop. 1.3. Yet the main subject of Ovid's poem (9-52) is the greed of his mistress and the tone changes distinctly between lines eight and nine. This particular imitation, then, creates a surprise effect at the beginning of *Am.* 1.10. The romantic tone of Ovid's first six lines contrasts sharply with the sordidness of the girl's conduct as it is described in the next forty lines. The Pro-pertian imitation leads us to expect an elegy of romantic mood, a mood which Ovid completely destroys after a few lines.[4]

The context of Prop. 1.3, in addition to adding to Ovid's surprise effect in *Am.* 1.10, provides a hint of the direction Ovid's elegy will ultimately take. *Am.* 1.10 does not end with the poet inveighing against the girl's greed. Rather, in an almost total reversal, Ovid agrees that a girl is entitled to gifts, whatever is within the means of her lover.

Am. 1.10.53-60, 63-64:

nec tamen indignum est a divite praemia posci:
   munera poscenti quod dare possit habet;
carpite de plenis pendentis vitibus uvas,
   praebeat Alcinoi poma benignus ager.
officium pauper numerat studiumque fidemque;
   quod quis habet, dominae conferat omne suae.
est quoque carminibus meritas celebrare puellas
   dos mea: quam volui, nota fit arte mea. ...
nec dare, sed pretium posci dedignor et odi;
   quod nego poscenti, desine velle, dabo.

---

[3] This is pointed out by L. C. Curran, "Ovid *Amores* 1.10" *Phoenix* 18 (1964) 314-18. In this excellent article, Curran discusses Ovid's use of Propertius at the beginning of *Am.* 1.10 as a way to increase the surprise inherent in the change of mood at line seven. A. Wlosok, "Die dritte Cynthia-Elegie des Properz" *Hermes* 95 (1967) 330-52 interprets the Propertian simile in a more complicated manner. She claims the three parallels represent different aspects of the situation which Propertius faces with Cynthia. Nevertheless, she does not deny the importance of the comparison for establishing a romantic mood. Neumann, 22, also notes this imitation but says that Ovid uses it simply "ut pulchritudinem Corinnae describat."

[4] Curran (*supra*) demonstrates (315) that the change in mood is made even more effective by Ovid's change at line 17 from the language of love to the language of commerce.

Ovid ends as he began on a note of romantic idealism. Gifts should be simple and the giving voluntary. This is exactly the scene described in Prop. 1.3. Cynthia is asleep and demands nothing, yet Propertius is so overwhelmed by her beauty and his feelings for her that he offers her gifts, albeit of a simple sort.

Prop. 1.3.21-26:

et modo solvebam nostra de fronte corollas
    ponebamque tuis, Cynthia, temporibus;
et modo gaudebam lapsos formare capillos;
    nunc furtiva cavis poma dabam manibus;
omniaque ingrato largibar munera somno,
    munera de prono saepe voluta sinu.

These gifts of garlands and apples are not only given unasked, they are not even appreciated by the sleeping Cynthia. Propertius is presenting us with free-hearted giving at its finest. When Cynthia does awaken, she makes no mention of the gifts but only complains of her loneliness. This is exactly the situation which Ovid's girl has precluded by her constant demands.

Given the background of Prop. 1.3, then, we should not be surprised by Ovid's sudden reversal at the end of his elegy.[5] The Propertian example of simple, voluntary gift giving is placed before us very succinctly by Ovid: *Quod quis habet, dominae conferat omne suae* (*Am.* 1.10.58). Prop. 1.3 is important both because it helps to heighten the effect of surprise brought about by Ovid's first change of mood (line 9) and because it foreshadows Ovid's second change of mood. When Ovid ultimately decides that unrequested, affordable gifts are all right, we have been prepared for his decision by the example of Propertius in 1.3.

Am. 2.17 is another elegy where Propertian imitation adds to the surprise of a change of mood. The first line of Ovid's elegy is a clear Propertian imitation.

Prop. 3.15.21:

si deus es, tibi turpe tuam servire puellam.

---

[5] There may be a direct echo of the simple Propertian gifts in Ovid's word *poma* (1.10.56). Propertius bestowed upon the sleeping Cynthia both apples and garlands (1.3.21-24).

Am. 2.17.1:

Si quis erit, qui turpe putet servire puellae.

The last lines of the two elegies also resemble each other:

Prop. 3.15.45-46:

fabula nulla tuas de nobis concitet auris:
te solam et lignis funeris ustus amem.

Am. 2.17.33-34:

nec nisi tu nostris cantabitur ulla libellis:
ingenio causas tu dabis una meo.

Prop. 3.15 is primarily a mythological narrative. Propertius tells the story of Dirce and Antiope to Cynthia, who has been acting harshly towards one of Propertius' previous loves, a woman named Lycinna.[6] The story is meant to persuade Cynthia to abide by Propertius' command:

Prop. 3.15.43:

at tu non meritam parcas vexare Lycinnam.

The mythological role assumed by each person at the beginning of the elegy has not changed when we reach the end. Cynthia is the cruel and heartless Dirce, Lycinna the persecuted Antiope. Dirce ultimately suffered for her haughty acts at the hands of Antiope's sons, and herein lies the message for Cynthia.

By his close imitation of Prop. 3.15 in the first line of *Am.* 2.17 Ovid establishes this myth as background for his own elegy. The cast of characters is somewhat different. Corinna is the violent one, but her victim is no longer another female but the poet himself. Ovid has given himself the role of the suffering Antiope.[7] Ovid's suffering, however, is not without its humorous aspect:

---

[6] For the latest discussion of Lycinna's identity and bibliography on this problem, see J. C. Yardley, "Propertius' Lycinna" *TAPA* 103 (1973) 429-34.

[7] Ovid emphasizes his position by echoing Propertius' word, *immitis*, a word used to describe Dirce's attitude towards Antiope (3.15.14). The word is used by Propertius only twice, here and at 4.11.13. Ovid uses *mitis* three times in the *Amores* but only in 2.17 does it mean "forgiving to inferiors" (see *ThLL* 8.1154.56). It is thus significant that Ovid says of himself:

atque utinam dominae miti quoque praeda fuissem.

(2.17.5)

Am. 2.17.9-10:

scilicet a speculi sumuntur imagine fastus,
    nec nisi conpositam se prius illa videt.

This playfulness in regard to his role as "sufferer" is the first indication that Ovid is not using the Propertian mythological background in a totally literal, serious fashion.

Prop. 3.15 is a serious elegy, for it reflects, on its most elementary
level, a power struggle. Propertius is struggling to gain the upper
hand over Cynthia and so tells her the story of Dirce. At the end
of the elegy he has not succeeded. Propertius is still in the position
of suppliant when he says:

Prop. 3.15.45-46:

fabula nulla tuas de nobis concitet auris:
    te solam et lignis funeris ustus amem.

In Ovid's poem, however, the power struggle ends quite differently.
Ovid is totally in charge and Corinna has become dependent on him.
"Dirce" has indeed been humbled and the instrument through which
this has been accomplished is poetry. The gift of poetry, it is
implied, is enough to decide any power struggle in favor of the poet.

Given the background of Prop. 3.15, this development is totally
unexpected. Ovid emphasizes the surprise effect very strongly by
juxtaposing distichs describing his total helplessness with distichs
reflecting on his very real power, the power of poetry.

Am. 2.17.23-30:

tu quoque me, mea lux, in quaslibet accipe leges;
    te deceat medio iura dedisse foro.
non tibi crimen ero nec quo laetere remoto;
    non erit hic nobis infitiandus amor.
sunt mihi pro magno felicia carmina censu,
    et multae per me nomen habere volunt:
novi aliquam, quae se circumferat esse Corinnam;
    ut fiat, quid non illa dedisse velit?

In one swift stroke, Ovid has reversed the mythological roles. He
is no longer the powerless, suffering Antiope, but has instead gained
the position of power within the relationship.[8] The change of mood

---

[8] It is tempting to equate Antiope's sons, who humble Dirce for her, with
Ovid's means of regaining power, his elegy. These poems are his "children"
and thus accomplish the same thing for him. This may, however, be carrying
the mythological equation too far.

becomes more emphatic when the elegy is read against the background of Prop. 3.15, where the balance of power does not change. The difference is succinctly summarized by the last lines of the two elegies. Although Ovid and Propertius are expressing the same sentiments, their tones are different. The Propertian line is almost a plea; the Ovidian line is a concession made from a position of power.

Another example of imitation which heightens the effect of a change of mood can be found in Ovid's propempticon, *Am.* 2.11. The propempticon theme was a traditional one in Latin elegy.[9] Propertius touched upon the theme several times but developed it most fully in 1.8. In *Am.* 2.11 Ovid has used the Propertian propempticon although he has by no means imitated as extensively as he did in his lena poem, another elegy written on a traditional theme.[10]

About halfway through *Am.* 2.11 Ovid has included the following imitation from Propertius' propempticon:

Prop. 1.8.17-18:

sed quocumque modo de me, periura, mereris,
  sit Galatea tuae non aliena viae.

Am. 2.11.33-34:

at si vana ferunt volucres mea dicta procellae,
  aequa tamen puppi sit Galatea tuae.

The figure of Galatea has provided Ovid with a way of linking his elegy to the earlier propempticon of Propertius.[11] Up to this point, both propemptica have developed along similar lines. After a short

---

[9] For a history of the propempticon theme, see K. Quinn, *Latin Explorations* (London, 1963) 239-42; F. Jäger, *Das antike Propemptikon und das 17 Gedicht des Paulinus von Nola* (diss. München, 1913) 4-36.

[10] For a discussion of *Am.* 1.8, Ovid's *lena* poem, see the end of Chapter IV. Neumann, 93-102, claims *Am.* 2.11 is based in its entirety on Prop. 1.8. His proof, however, depends on similar themes (such as a description of the dangers of the sea).

[11] Such an appeal to Galatea is found in no other extant Latin propempticon. Even if she figures in a lost propempticon (for the fragments of Cinna's propempticon *cf.* Morel, *FPL* 87-88), the wording *sit Galatea tuae* which Ovid has borrowed directly from Propertius would force the association of *Am.* 2.11 and Prop. 1.8. W. Görler, "Ovids Propemptikon (*Amores* 2.11)" *Hermes* 93 (1965) 338-47 says of this imitation: ". . . es kann keinem Zweifel unterliegen dass Ovid sein Zitat erkannt wissen wollte" (344).

introduction in which Ovid curses the invention of ships and Propertius airs his hurt feelings over the rival who is enticing Cynthia to put to sea, each poet tries to dissuade his girl from embarking on the perilous ocean voyage. Eventually each abandons this attempt and offers best wishes for the journey if the girl will indeed persevere. In both elegies, the Galatea distich marks this change in feeling.

Ovid now makes use of this Propertian background to introduce a subtle but effective change of mood. Propertius follows his wishes for Cynthia's safe journey with six lines (21-26) in which he predicts his faithfulness to her after she sails. Then suddenly, whether in the same poem or in a separate but related one, Propertius breaks into a passage of unrestrained joy because Cynthia has decided to remain at home after all.[12] This tone is echoed in *Am.* 2.11 where Ovid, too, almost immediately after the Galatea verse introduces a joyous passage about Corinna's return (43-52).

The Ovidian passage, however, is very ironic. Propertius' joy is real, Ovid's is imaginary. Corinna, unlike Cynthia, has not agreed to stay. Ovid is simply imagining what might happen when Corinna finally does return from her voyage. Yet the parallel structure of the elegies up to this point leads to the expectation of an Ovidian ending similar to the Propertian one. Ovid has used imitation as a means to make his imaginary "happiness" all the more poignant and ironic.

The importance of the imaginary for Ovid's purposes in *Am.* 2.11 is demonstrated in other ways also. The most obvious of these is an imitation of Tibullus with which Ovid concludes his poem.

Tib. 1.3.93-94:
hoc precor, hunc illum nobis Aurora nitentem
 Luciferum roseis candida portet equis.

Am. 2.11.55-56:
haec mihi quam primum caelo nitidissimus alto
 Lucifer admisso tempora portet equo.

---

[12] For arguments and bibliography on whether Prop. 1.8 should be one poem or two, see P. J. Enk (Chapter 1, note 5: *Liber Primus*, part 2) 74-75; also K. Jäger, *Zweigliedrige Gedichte und Gedichtpaare bei Properz und in Ovids Amores* (diss. Tübingen, 1967) 47-55. Jäger (31-33) claims that *Am.* 2.11 and 2.12 are a poetic pair based on Prop. 1.8 and 1.8B. There is little evidence for this, however, except for the general similarity of tone and the word *vicimus* which appears in the second line of each of the "triumph poems."

The Tibullan distich both ends an elegy and, more important, marks the end of a flight of fancy. Tibullus is imagining himself coming home and Delia meeting him while in reality he is deathly ill in Phaeacia. Ovid's use of this imitation at the end of his poem, then, can only emphasize the imaginary quality of his own description.

The imaginary joy of the end of the poem is also hinted at by Ovid early in *Am.* 2.11. At this point, he still has hopes of dissuading Corinna from the voyage. Yet very subtly, by including an imitation from Prop. 1.8B, Ovid foreshadows what he will develop in detail in the second half of his poem.

Prop. 1.8B.29-30:

falsa licet cupidus deponat gaudia livor:
    destitit ire novas Cynthia nostra vias.

Am. 2.11.7-8:

ecce fugit notumque torum sociosque Penates
    fallacisque vias ire Corinna parat.

The Propertian pentameter is a joyful announcement that Cynthia has decided to remain at home. The decision has been made (*destitit*) and consequently, the world of the imaginary (*falsa ... gaudia...*) is banished by Propertius from this very real reunion. Ovid's situation is entirely different, as the verb *parat* indicates. Nothing has been decided in his favor, and indeed *falsa gaudia* will soon (line 37) be all he has. This imitation, then, effectively hints at what is to come, the contrast between real and imaginary joy, so important for establishing the poignant mood at the end of *Am.* 2.11.[13]

Up to this point, we have discussed imitations which affect the changes of mood within single elegies. We must now turn to changes of mood which occur between the two poems of Ovidian poetic pairs. While the poetic pair form did not originate with Ovid, he used it extensively in the *Amores*.[14] We can number six poetic pairs

---

[13] The poignancy of the situation, the bleakness of an imaginary reunion, is increased when Ovid admits that he knows he is only pretending (53-54). All of the imitations which emphasize Ovid's pretence thus contribute to the pathetic quality of the end of the poem.

[14] See Jäger (*supra*, note 12) 46-99 for a discussion of poetic pairs in Propertius.

among the fifty poems of the collection.[15] Every one of these pairs demonstrates a distinct change of tone at the beginning of the second poem. Indeed, change of mood is so important within the poetic pairs of the *Amores* that they have been termed "little dramas in two scenes."[16] Several of these pairs contain Propertian imitations which emphasize the change of mood.

The simplest example of Propertian imitation within a poetic pair is found in *Am.* 1.12. In this case Ovid establishes a Propertian background which contrasts with the tone of his own elegy.[17]

Prop. 3.23.15-20:

aut dixit: 'Venies hodie, cessabimus una:
   hospitium tota nocte paravit Amor,'
et quaecumque volens reperit non stulta puella
   garrula, cum blandis dicitur hora dolis.
me miserum, his aliquis rationem scribit avarus
   et ponit duras inter ephemeridas!

Am. 1.12.23-26:

aptius hae capiant vadimonia garrula cerae,
   quas aliquis duro cognitor ore legat;
inter ephemeridas melius tabulasque iacerent,
   in quibus absumptas fleret avarus opes.

Am. 1.12 is the second poem in Ovid's pair. In 1.11 the poet has dispatched a slave, Nape, with a message for Corinna, and indeed, 1.11 ends with talk of suitable rewards for the tablets:

Am. 1.11.27-28:

subscribam 'Veneri fidas sibi Naso ministras
   dedicat. At nuper vile fuistis acer.'

---

[15] I count as poetic pairs *Am.* 1.11, 12; 2.2,3; 7, 8; 9, 9B; 13, 14; 3.11, 11B. This follows the design of L. Müller, who divided 2.9 and 3.11 and bracketed 3.5 (see *Philol.* 11 [1856] 89 ff.). We then have fifteen elegies in Books I and III, twenty in Book II. For definitive arguments against the Ovidian authorship of *Am.* 3.5, see E. J. Kenney, "On the *Somnium* Attributed to Ovid," *Agon* 3 (1969) 1-14. For bibliography concerning the division of *Am.* 2.9, see Jäger (*supra*, note 12) 148-49; concerning *Am.* 3.11, Jäger 142.

[16] Jäger (*supra*, note 12) 39. His actual words are "Kleindramen in zwei Szenen."

[17] Neumann, 59-63, discusses this imitation and the variations Ovid has made on his Propertian original. He does not, however, discuss Ovid's possible motives for making these changes.

In *Am.* 1.12, however, Ovid is plunged into deep despair. The tablets have not been successful in their mission. The disappointment of the poet finds its outlet in the curses which Ovid liberally heaps upon the tablets at the end of 1.12.

In the very first line of his elegy, Ovid reminds the reader of Prop. 3.23. He then proceeds to contrast his attitude with that of his predecessor. In Prop. 3.23 the poet is grief stricken precisely because his tablets have been lost. They, unlike Ovid's, have customarily enjoyed success on their mission of persuasion. Propertius even goes so far as to offer a reward for their return:

Prop. 3.23.21-22:

quas si quis mihi rettulerit, donabitur auro:
    quis pro divitiis ligna retenta velit?

Ovid's tablets, on the other hand, have not been lost but he himself tells them:

Am. 1.12.7:

ite hinc, difficiles, funebria ligna, tabellae.

Earlier Propertius has expressed fear that his tablets may have fallen into the hands of a miser for service in keeping accounts. In a very close imitation (25-26) Ovid wishes this very thing would happen to his tablets.

The contrast between these two poems, then, effectively heightens the feeling of bitterness which Ovid is attempting to create in *Am.* 1.12.[18] The happy relationship which Propertius enjoyed with his tablets makes Ovid's insults and imprecations all the more shocking. Insofar as the imitations of Prop. 3.23 help to increase the bitterness in *Am.* 1.12, they are also contributing to the effectiveness of the change of mood between *Am.* 1.11 and 1.12. The tone of *Am.* 1.11 is one of confident hope. The despair of *Am.* 1.12 is totally different and surprising. Imitation is one means by which Ovid strengthens this contrast of tone.[19]

---

[18] I. M. Le M. Du Quesnay (Chapter I, note 13) in his long discussion of this poetic pair (30-40) makes note of this particular imitation and the contrast Ovid is creating. His emphasis, however, is different. He concludes: "Again the allusion is used to reveal that Ovid's *persona* is a caricature, a parody of the Propertian lover" (39).

[19] For other ways in which Ovid strengthens the contrast of tones, see Du Quesnay's discussion of *Am.* 1.11,12 mentioned in the note above. While I do not agree that *Am.* 1.11.25-28 refers specifically to Prop. 2.14a. 23-28, Du Quesnay discusses two Horatian imitations which effectively contribute to the tone of hopeful expectation in *Am.* 1.11 (33-34).

Propertian imitation contributes to the change of mood in a
different way in *Am.* 2.13. In this elegy Ovid is praying for Corinna's
return to health after her abortion. His true feelings about her act
are expressed in *Am.* 2.14, the second poem of this pair, where he
delivers an impassioned tirade against abortion and those women
who use it. Ovid even goes so far as to include Corinna among the
guilty, should she ever do it again: *et satis est: poenam culpa secunda
ferat* (2.14.44).

Even in *Am.* 2.13, where Ovid is primarily concerned with
Corinna's recovery, there are hints of impending change of mood.
This is accomplished through the use of imitations which emphasize
the issue of abortion. These imitations are taken from Prop. 2.28.[20]

Prop. 2.28B.41-46:

si non unius, quaeso, miserere duorum!
    vivam, si vivet; si cadet illa, cadam.
pro quibus optatis sacro me carmine damno:
    scribam ego 'Per magnum est salva puella Iovem';
ante tuosque pedes illa ipsa operata sedebit,
    narrabitque sedens longa pericla sua.

Am. 2.13.15-18, 25-26:

huc adhibe vultus et in una parce duobus:
    nam vitam dominae tu dabis, illa mihi.
saepe tibi sedit certis operata diebus,
    qua tingit laurus Gallica turma tuas ...
adiciam titulum 'Servata Naso Corinna':
    tu modo fac titulo muneribusque locum.

Propertius, like Ovid, is praying for the life of his mistress who
lies sick.[21] We are not, however, told the exact nature of Cynthia's

---

[20] For a discussion of the problems surrounding the division of Prop.
2.28, see U. Knoche, "Gedanken und Vorschläge zur Interpretation von
Properzens Gedicht II.28" in Eisenhut (ed.), *Antike Lyrik* (Darmstadt,
1970) 379-401, particularly 379-84. (This article originally appeared in
Miscellanea Properziana. Atti dell' Accad. Properziana del Subasio V. 5
[1957].); Jäger (*supra*, note 12) 56-57.

[21] The idea of saving two lives by sparing one is common in ancient
literature. For detail, see E. Bréguet, "*In una parce duobus*: Thème et
Clichés," *Hommages à L. Hermann, Collection Latomus* 44 (1960) 205-14.
The claim of imitation here is based not on this theme but on the use and
position of specific words in Ovid's poem, namely *duobus, illa*, and *operata
sedit*.

illness. Propertius makes some attempt in 2.28A to connect it with false swearing (lines 5-8) but we are never given a medical diagnosis as we are in the first line of Ovid's poem.[22] Anyone familiar with Propertius' elegy knows that Cynthia did indeed recover and, in fact, in the lines immediately following this passage, Propertius offers thanks to Persephone for sparing his mistress. Cynthia recovers partly, we must suppose, on the basis of the promise Propertius makes to Jove for her. Cynthia, when she is well, will perform sacrifices. In Ovid's imitation Corinna has already performed religious duties, albeit to Isis rather than to Jove. Corinna's piety is thus established by the simple change of Propertius' *operata sedebit* to *sedit operata*.

It is at this point that Ovid begins to use the Propertian background to emphasize the unsavory nature of Corinna's illness. Immediately after his invocation to Isis, Ovid calls upon Ilithyia, helper of women in childbirth (19-22). It is to this goddess that Ovid will offer the credit for saving Corinna. Propertius, on the other hand, will dedicate his inscription about Cynthia's salvation to Jove. The contrast between the two deities can only serve to remind the reader of Corinna's abortion—a beautifully ironic touch, following as it does the establishment of her piety.

This contrast becomes even more vivid if we look at the end of Prop. 2.28C. Propertius now offers credit for Cynthia's recovery to another deity, the virgin goddess Diana.

Prop. 2.28C.59-60:

tu quoniam es, mea lux, magno dimissa periclo,
  munera Dianae debita redde choros.

This can be contrasted to a line near the end of Ovid's poem:

ipse feram ante tuos munera vota pedes (24).

Ovid's *munera vota* correspond to the *munera debita* of Propertius, but once again, Ovid is speaking to Ilithyia. The contrast is no longer between Ilithyia and a neutral figure like Jove, but between the goddess of childbirth and a goddess of virginity. Again, the whole

---

[22] Ovid baldly states:

Dum labefactat onus gravidi temeraria ventris,
  in dubio vitae lassa Corinna iacet.
               (2.13.1-2)

question of the abortion is brought to our attention by this minor change.

Ovid's imitations of Prop. 2.28 thus contribute to *Am.* 2.13-14 by keeping the issue of abortion and Ovid's reaction to it constantly before the reader. Even as we sympathize with Corinna, we are aware that her troubles were self-inflicted. The subtle barbs directed at Corinna through the implied comparison with Cynthia are indications of the anger of the poet. Much as he prays for Corinna's recovery he is not at all pleased by her behavior. It is no surprise, then, when in 2.14 Ovid stops suppressing his anger and begins to castigate the now recovering Corinna.

In *Am.* 2.13 Ovid has used imitation to increase the unity of his poetic pair. Although the subject in both poems is the same, the point of view from which it is treated is entirely different. Yet the different viewpoint has been foreshadowed by imitations placed near the end of the first elegy. This was a technique Ovid used often in the poetic pairs, in fact in three out of the six. A poetic pair was meant to surprise through the introduction of a change of tone at the beginning of the second elegy, but the pair was also a single whole with a need for unity between the two parts. Subtle imitations of the type just discussed were an excellent means for achieving the second goal without destroying the effect of surprise.[23]

In *Am.* 2.9 and 2.9b Ovid uses this same device. In the first poem, near the end, he hints through imitation at the tone which he will adopt in the second.[24] In the first twenty-four lines of *Am.* 2.9 Ovid addresses Cupid and begs him for a respite from love. At line 25, however, the tone completely changes. The poet now announces that even were the respite to be granted, he wouldn't accept it. Indeed, he concludes 2.9b by asking Cupid to continue to rule over his heart.

Immediately preceding the change of mood in these two poems, Ovid has included an obvious Propertian imitation.[25]

---

[23] Ovid used other means to achieve this unity also. For example, Jäger (*supra*, note 12) 22, points out the unifying effect of the word *pugna* in *Am.* 2.13 and 14. Ovid uses the word in line 28 of the first poem and line 8 of the second.

[24] There has been some dispute on the question of dividing this poem (see *supra*, note 15). The fact that Ovid used Propertian imitation in 2.9 in exactly the same way as in 2.13, strengthens the argument for dividing the poem after line 24.

[25] Neumann, 34-37, expounds on the derivation of *Am.* 2.9 and 2.9b from Prop. 2.12. I do not find his alleged imitations convincing.

Prop. 2.25.5-10:

miles depositis annosus secubat armis,
    grandaevique negant ducere aratra boves,
putris et in vacua requiescit navis harena,
    et vetus in templo bellica parma vacat:
at me ab amore tuo deducet nulla senectus,
    sive ego Tithonus sive ego Nestor ero.

Am. 2.9.19-24:

fessus in acceptos miles deducitur agros,
    mittitur in saltus carcere liber equus,
longaque subductam celant navalia pinum,
    tutaque deposito poscitur ense rudis:
me quoque, qui totiens merui sub amore puellae,
    defunctum placide vivere tempus erat.

This imitation achieves two separate effects. First, Ovid has
created a minor "surprise." He follows the Propertian structure
for four lines and then in the last distich says exactly the opposite of
what Propertius says. Propertius claims that unlike the retired
soldier, etc., he wants no rest. Ovid, by altering the *at me* of his
predecessor to *me quoque*, leaves us with the opposite impression.
He does indeed want a rest from love.

This imitation, however, also indicates the direction the second
poem of the pair will take. Ovid begins *Am.* 2.9b on the same note
struck by Propertius in 2.25.9-10.

Am. 2.9b.25-26:

'Vive' deus 'posito' si quis mihi dicat 'amore,'
    deprecer: usque adeo dulce puella malum est.

The reader, who has just absorbed the impact of Ovid's direct
contradiction of Propertius, would at first be doubly surprised at
this abrupt and total change of tone between 2.9 and 2.9b. Yet
this is, ultimately, a return to the Propertian position on love, as
it is expressed in Prop. 2.25. The imitation thus operates as a hint
because of its Propertian context. It subtly foreshadows the new
tone which will be introduced in *Am.* 2.9b.

The same kind of unifying hint through imitation has been
included by Ovid at the end of *Am.* 3.11. In *Am.* 3.11 Ovid claims

that he is through with love forever.[26] He has suffered enough and
indeed, he even catalogues the trials he has endured at the hands
of his mistress (9-26). In 3.11b, however, the tone changes completely. Ovid confesses that he is unable to leave his mistress. Her
hold on him has more power than he had realized.

Am. 3.11b.33-34:

Luctantur pectusque leve in contraria tendunt
    hac amor, hac odium; sed, puto, vincit amor.

Am. 3.11 concludes with four lines modelled on Prop. 3.24.[27]

Prop. 3.24.15-18:

ecce coronatae portum tetigere carinae,
    traiectae Syrtes, ancora iacta mihi est.
nunc demum vasto fessi resipiscimus aestu,
    vulneraque ad sanum nunc coiere mea.

Am. 3.11.29-32:

iam mea votiva puppis redimita corona
    lenta tumescentes aequoris audit aquas.
desine blanditias et verba potentia quondam
    perdere: non ego sum stultus, ut ante fui.

Prop. 3.24 is an elegy in which Propertius is repudiating Cynthia.
Together with 3.25 it forms his farewell to his mistress and the
conclusion to his first three books of elegy.[28] Prop. 3.24 represents

---

[26] While the manuscripts show these fifty-two lines as one continuous
poem, it is now generally divided (*supra*, note 15). Again, as with *Am.*
2.9 and 2.9b, the unifying imitation at the end of the first poem strengthens
the argument for division (see note 24, above).

[27] Neumann, 74-79, claims that *Am.* 3.11 was based on Prop. 3.24 and
3.25. He points up a number of similar themes in the two poems. While I
agree with him about Prop. 3.24, I base the claim for imitation here on the
image of the garlanded ship reaching port. This exact image is found only
here in the Ovidian corpus. On two other occasions, Ovid speaks of a garlanded ship, but does not emphasize the end of the voyage (*Met.* 15.696,
Fast. 4.335). For other imitations in *Am.* 3.11, see N. Gross, "Ovid, *Amores*
3.11A and B: A Literary Mélange" *CJ* 71 (1975-6) 152-60.

[28] FLPDV write these two elegies as one. Some editors have followed
these manuscripts (see Smyth [Chapter IV, note 14] 122). I agree with the
editors who divide the poems. I do not think Ovid would have imitated as he
did if Prop. 3.25—an elegy much more emphatic about the finality of the
separation—were truly a part of Prop. 3.24.

Propertius' first step towards separation; 3.25 brings the affair to an emphatic and angry end.

While Propertius at the end of 3.24 seems convinced of his freedom from Cynthia's power (15-20), in its middle section (9-14) he reviews the tremendous difficulties he experienced while attempting to free himself in the past.

Prop. 3.24.9-14:

quod mihi non patrii poterant avertere amici,
    eluere aut vasto Thessala saga mari,
hoc ego non ferro, non igne coactus, et ipsa
    naufragus Aegaea—vera fatebor—aqua:
correptus saevo Veneris torrebar aeno;
    vinctus eram versas in mea terga manus.

It is, of course, the difficulty of escaping from love which is to become Ovid's theme in *Am.* 3.11b. The reader who is familiar with Prop. 3.24 will not find Ovid's inability to act on his resolve totally unexpected. The choice of Propertian model for the end of *Am.* 3.11 foreshadows the mood of *Am.* 3.11b.[29]

In the poetic pairs, then, Ovid's use of Propertian imitation is connected with the change of mood which is the hallmark of this type of poetic composition. In three of the pairs Propertian imitation helps to promote unity between the two elegies. The "hint" at the end of the first poem prepares the reader for the tone of the second. In one pair imitation contributes directly to the contrast between the first and second poems.[30]

Within individual elegies which exhibit a change of tone, the creation of a surprise effect was clearly Ovid's primary goal in his use of Propertian imitation. In these elegies, even more than in the

---

[29] A similar effect may be operating at *Am.* 3.11.5: *vicimus et domitum pedibus calcamus Amorem.* I. M. Le M. Du Quesnay (Chapter I, note 13) says this line is probably an echo of Prop. 1.1.4 (23-24). If so, it is significant that Prop. 1.1 also deals with the difficulties of escaping from love once it has entered one's life.

[30] The three pairs which contain imitations of the first type (*Am.* 2.13, 14; 2.9, 9b; 3.11, 11b) are all serious Ovidian elegies. The other three pairs (*Am.* 1.11, 12; 2.2, 3; 2.7, 8) are much lighter. There are no Propertian imitations at all in *Am.* 2.2, 3 and 7, 8, and in 1.11, 12 Ovid imitates Propertius to increase the impact of his disappointment through contrast with his predecessor. This may indicate that unity was uppermost in serious Ovidian pairs, surprise in the lighter ones.

pairs, Ovid has used imitation for a variety of reasons. While the motive for which he introduces the surprise effect may vary from poem to poem, the effectiveness of his use of imitation remains constant. In every case Ovid adds some subtle nuance to his own elegy. In both the poetic pairs and the individual elegies discussed above, Ovid has once again demonstrated his artistry by his creative use of Propertian imitation.

CHAPTER SIX

OVID'S FAREWELL: THE THIRD BOOK OF THE *AMORES*

Ovid's use of Propertian imitation in Book Three is somewhat different from what we find in the other two books of the *Amores*. In general, the imitations in this book contribute to Ovid's goals of divorcing himself from the writing of love elegy and devoting himself to poetry of a weightier, more serious sort. In the first elegy of the third book, this goal is set forth through the debate between the figures of Tragedy and Elegy. This poem, which takes much from Prop. 3.3, nevertheless deviates from the earlier programmatic poem in its ending.[1] In Prop. 3.3, the elegist is warned by the Muses to continue writing love elegy. Ovid's poem ends with a compromise solution.

Am. 3.1.67-70:

'exiguum vati concede, Tragoedia, tempus:
    tu labor aeternus; quod petit illa, breve est.'
mota dedit veniam. teneri properentur Amores,
    dum vacat: a tergo grandius urguet opus.

The reader thus enters upon Book Three forewarned that it constitutes Ovid's elegiac "swansong." He may not, however, be prepared for the subtle ways in which Ovid emphasizes the impending change in his literary goals. To give just one example, in *Am.* 3.1 Ovid reminds us of the possibilities offered by serious elegy. This is accomplished through imitation which brings to mind the Propertian image of the doves of Venus dipping their bills in water which inspires serious poetry (Prop. 3.3.31-32). One immediately thinks of Propertius' fourth book, that collection of mythological and aetiological poems which Propertius himself calls the work of the "Roman Callimachus" (4.1.64). Ovid was to produce serious elegy of this type in the guise of the *Fasti*, and he includes in Book Three several poems which can only be considered previews of this later work.[2] These elegies are not primarily about love but center

---

[1] See the discussion of *Am.* 3.1, Chapter II, pages 17-21.

[2] Foremost amongst these are *Am.* 3.10 and 3.13, elegies concerning a festival of Ceres and a festival of Juno, respectively. That these poems are previews of the *Fasti* is the view of F. W. Lenz, "Junofest (Ovid *Amores* III.13)" *Fabula* I (1957-58) 255-262. He also emphasizes Ovid's debt to Callimachus' *Aetia*, particularly in regard to 3.10.

around mythological narrative or the description of religious ritual.

Ovid also does everything possible in Book Three to convince the reader that his own love affair has soured and is reaching its end. Since Cupid's arrow caused Ovid to begin writing love elegy (*Am.* 1.1) it is only natural that once he is no longer in love, love elegy will cease to occupy his time. Propertian imitations, judiciously used, play a role in emphasizing how hopeless Ovid's romantic situation has become. They also serve to underline the theme of death and the tone of gloom that pervade so many of these last elegies of the *Amores*.

Yet as the reader progresses from the programmatic poem that opens the book, there is no immediate hint of what is to come. *Am.* 3.2, 3.3 and 3.4 are typical Ovidian love elegies which could have been included in Books One and Two just as easily as in Book Three. *Am.* 3.2 is a long, didactic discourse on picking up a girl at the races; *Am.* 3.3 treats the topic of perjury by pretty girls; 3.4, in a complete turnabout from 2.19, chides the jealous husband for guarding his wife.[3]

If we disregard *Am.* 3.5, the so-called *Somnium*, as non-Ovidian, the first elegy which is noticeably different in its subject matter is *Am.* 3.6.[4] Ovid begins with a love interest:

Am. 3.6.1-2:

Amnis harundinibus limosas obsite ripas,
    ad dominam propero: siste parumper aquas.

At the end (85-106), he will return to this theme. In between, however, he is concerned with mythological material (23-84), and most specifically with the long narrative story of the River Anio falling in love with Rhea Silvia, mother of Romulus and Remus (45-84). This elegy, then, is not completely divorced from the idea of love,

---

[3] *Am.* 3.2 contains no Propertian imitations. Because of the didactic nature of this piece, it is possible to consider it a preview of the *Ars* (see E. Thomas, "Ovid at the Races. *Amores* III.2; *Ars amatoria* I.135-164" in *Hommages à M. Renard* I [Brussels, 1969] 710-24). Propertian imitations in *Am.* 3.3 and 3.4 have been discussed in Chapter III, pages 33-34; 38-40.

[4] For the non-Ovidian authorship of *Am.* 3.5, see Kenney (Chapter V, note 15). The acceptance of this elegy as a part of Book III can perhaps be explained by the number of elegies in the third book which differ substantially from the "typical" Ovidian love elegy.

but the emphasis has shifted. We are not so much concerned with the poet's own love as with the telling of the tale.[5]

Within Ovid's mythological narrative there are some important imitations taken from Prop. 4.7, a rather strange poem about Cynthia revisiting Propertius after her death. Ovid's references to Prop. 4.7 call attention to Cynthia's instructions concerning her grave.

Prop. 4.7.79-86:

pelle hederam tumulo, mihi quae praegnante corymbo
    mollia contortis alligat ossa comis.
ramosis Anio qua pomifer incubat arvis,
    et numquam Herculeo numine pallet ebur,
hic carmen media dignum me scribe columna,
    sed breve, quod currens vector ab urbe legat:
'Hic Tiburtina iacet aurea Cynthia terra:
    accessit ripae laus, Aniene, tuae.'

A close imitation is found in the opening lines of Ovid's Anio narrative.[6]

Am. 3.6.45-46:

nec te praetereo, qui per cava saxa volutans
    Tiburis Argei pomifer arva rigas.

Clearly Ovid wants to associate the Anio, as described in Am. 3.6, with the Anio described by Cynthia in Prop. 4.7.81.

Ovid has made the connection between Am. 3.6 and the Propertian passage even stronger. He, like Propertius, mentions Hercules (Am. 3.6.36). He also opts for the archaic form when he gives the name of the river.

---

[5] The narrative of Am. 3.6 prefigures the Fasti. As R. Heinze has pointed out ("Ovids elegische Erzählung" in Vom Geist des Römertums [Teubner, 1960] 338-403), narrative in the Fasti generally humanizes divinity and emphasizes "soft" feelings like pity. Ovid's elegiac and epic narrative are compared by B. Otis, Ovid as an Epic Poet[2] (Cambridge, 1970) 49-59.

[6] Imitation here is demonstrated by the use of pomifer as an epithet for a river. Although pomifer as an epithet for the Anio is attested by the manuscript tradition of Propertius, some editors have felt the need to emend (see Smyth [Chapter IV, note 14] 150). However, considering Propertian imagery in general and the liberties he took with -fer compound adjectives (see Tränkle [Chapter I, note 15] 58), this use of pomifer does not seem objectionable.

Am. 3.6.51-52 :

hanc Anien rapidis animosus vidit ab undis
raucaque de mediis sustulit ora vadis.

In classical times, *Anio* was the preferred nominative form of the name of this river while *Anien* was retained in the oblique cases.[7] Ovid's use of *Anien* as a nominative, then, was unusual, but understandable if he wanted to link his Anio to the one in Prop. 4.7 (line 86-*Aniene*).

This elegy, then, supplies an important clue to Ovid's changing interests. Not only has Ovid made mythological narrative rather than the beloved mistress the center of this poem, he has used Propertian imitation to remind the reader of a mistress who is dead. The River Anio, described in Propertian terms, is the vehicle through which this is accomplished. Although the river is a lover in his own right and thus a fitting subject for Ovid's mythological narrative, his close association with the dead Cynthia adds certain sinister overtones to his appearance in a purported love elegy. At best, he is an ambiguous figure. It is not surprising, then, that ultimately he refuses to listen to Ovid's pleas and becomes the cause of the poet-lover's separation from his girl friend. Ovid's failure to successfully complete his tryst coupled with the introduction (through imitation) of the dead Cynthia into *Am.* 3.6 produces a mood which is very negative towards love.[8]

This negative attitude towards love reappears in *Am.* 3.7 in a different guise. In this elegy Ovid spends 84 lines lamenting his sexual impotence.[9] Never before has Ovid mentioned any such problem. Indeed, in *Am.* 2.10.23-28 he boasted of his unflagging sexual abilities, and in 1.5 we observed the foreplay to a very successful encounter with Corinna. So why has the lover-poet now developed sexual problems? He is once again pointing to the end of his involvement in traditional love elegy, this time by presenting

---

[7] See Lewis and Short, s.v. *Anio.*

[8] The figure of Ilia, the girl loved by the River Anio, also contributes to this negative mood. Although she eventually surrenders herself to the river, we are never told that she improved her lot by this act (79-82).

[9] *Am.* 3.7 has often been relegated to the shadowy realm of "bad taste." Typical is the comment of Newman (Chapter II, note 1) 103: "It is useless to defend it (3.7) by talking about 'frankness.' Ovid is not writing his 'true confession' for the Sunday newspapers, he is cold bloodedly making up a scene to titillate."

himself as a failure. In *Am*. 3.7, Ovid the lover is a physical failure. In *Am*. 3.8, Ovid the lover is a poetic failure.

Propertian imitations in *Am*. 3.7 are limited to short echoes which contrast with the more conventional attitudes of sexual ability expressed by the older poet.

Prop. 1.9.29-32:

qui non ante patet, donec manus attigit ossa:
  quisquis es, assiduas a fuge blanditias!
illis et silices et possint cedere quercus,
  nedum tu possis, spiritus iste levis.

Am. 3.7.57-60:

illa graves potuit quercus adamantaque durum
  surdaque blanditiis saxa movere suis:
digna movere fuit certe vivosque virosque,
  sed neque tum vixi nec vir, ut ante, fui.

The irony here is immediately apparent. The power of the girl's *blanditiae* is discussed by each poet. Propertius expresses the attitude that nothing and certainly no man can withstand such powers. Ovid echoes this sentiment and then promptly turns around and tells us that he, to his horror, withstood them. The contrast with Propertius increases the force of Ovid's self-deprecation. He wants to emphasize his total failure as a lover and the use of imitation which creates contrast adds extra strength to his self-loathing.

It is for a similar reason that Ovid makes reference to Thamyras.[10]

Prop. 2.22A.19-22:

me licet et Thamyrae cantoris fata sequantur,
  numquam ad formosas, invide, caecus ero.
sed tibi si exilis videor tenuatus in artus,
  falleris: haud umquam est culta labore Venus.

Am. 3.7.61-62:

quid iuvet, ad surdas si cantet Phemius aures?
  quid miserum Thamyran picta tabella iuvat?

---

[10] Ovid refers to Thamyras only three times in his entire corpus—here, *Ars* 3.399, *Ib*. 272.

Propertius' reference to this blind Thracian poet is directly followed by a statement explaining his own more than adequate sexual powers. Ovid's inclusion of Thamyras in his poem about impotence can only be a deliberate reminder of the atypical nature of his physical state. The traditional poet-lover is more than sexually adequate, like Propertius in 2.22A. Again, the sense of failure is intensified.

Am. 3.8 continues the theme of the failure of Ovid as a poet-lover. In 3.8. a rich rival has usurped Ovid's place with his beloved, a common enough theme in elegy.[11] Ovid's treatment of the theme is interesting, however, in that at the beginning of the poem he equates his failure with his poetic talent.

Am. 3.8.1-8:

Et quisquam ingenuas etiam nunc suspicit artes
    aut tenerum dotes carmen habere putat?
ingenium quondam fuerat pretiosius auro,
    at nunc barbaria est grandis habere nihil.
cum pulchre dominae nostri placuere libelli,
    quo licuit libris, non licet ire mihi;
cum bene laudavit, laudato ianua clausa est:
    turpiter huc illuc ingeniosus eo.

Love elegy is no longer of any use in winning Ovid girls. Yet he has stated earlier that it was for precisely this reason that he was writing love elegy.[12] If his *ingenium* no longer opens closed doors, Ovid has one more reason for abandoning love elegy and moving on to other types of poetry.

The bitterness which Ovid feels in regard to the triumph of wealth over poetry is emphasized by the one Propertian imitation in *Am.* 3.8. Near the end of his elegy, Ovid says about wealthy men:

---

[11] For example, Prop. 2.16; Tib. 1.9, 2.4.
[12] One need only look to *Am.* 2.1 or 3.1:

clausit amica fores: ego cum Iove fulmen omisi;
    excidit ingenio Iuppiter ipse meo.
Iuppiter, ignoscas: nil me tua tela iuvabant;
    clausa tuo maius ianua fulmen habet.
blanditias elegosque levis, mea tela, resumpsi:
    mollierunt duras lenia verba fores.
                     (*Am.* 2.1.17-22)
quam tu non poteris duro reserare cothurno,
    haec est blanditiis ianua laxa meis.
                     (3.1.45-6)

Am. 3.8.57-62:

omnia possideant: illis Campusque Forumque
   serviat, hi pacem crudaque bella gerant;
tantum ne nostros avidi liceantur amores
   et (satis est) aliquid pauperis esse sinant.
at nunc, exaequet tetricas licet illa Sabinas,
   imperat ut captae, qui dare multa potest.

This passage is based on a Propertian elegy whose context is important for Ovid's purposes here. Indeed, the second half of the last pentameter is an exact imitation.

Prop. 2.26B.21-28:

Nunc admirentur quod tam mihi pulchra puella
   serviat et tota dicar in urbe potens!
non, si Cambysae redeant et flumina Croesi,
   dicat 'De nostro surge, poeta, toro.'
nam mea cum recitat, dicit se odisse beatos:
   carmina tam sancte nulla puella colit.
multum in amore fides, multum constantia prodest.
   qui dare multa potest, multa et amare potest? [13]

If we assume that the first *multa* of line 28 refers to the wealth implied in line 23, we have a situation which is exactly opposite the one of *Am.* 3.8.[14] Propertius first states the conventional view of the power of love poetry. In the matter of winning girls, it is more powerful than wealth. He ends by asking whether the rich man will win his girl. The answer, of course, is no.

Ovid has thus used this Propertian imitation to create contrast which emphasizes the hopelessness of his own situation. His powers of poetry have totally failed and his girl has gone off with the rich

---

[13] For conjectures about the arrangement of lines in Prop. 2.26, see Smyth (Chapter IV, note 14) 67-68. Most editors feel that these eight lines form a unit (exceptions include Carutti, Postgate, Birt). The last pentameter (28) has been condemned by some (Broekhuyzen) but the line is ably defended by G. Luck, "Beiträge zum Text der römischen Elegiker" *RhM* 105 (1962) 337-51, see particularly 343. He also argues for retaining the order of 21-28. Rothstein was the first to punctuate this line as a question. This makes sense in view of Ovid's imitation.

[14] Other interpretations have been offered, among them that of Luck (*supra*, note 13) who would have *multa* refer to *fides* and *constantia*.

soldier. In fact, by beginning his pentameter (62) *imperat ut captae*
..., Ovid emphasizes the soldier's total and complete control. This
underlines even more strongly his own failure. Just as Ovid's sexual
powers left him in 3.7, here the amatory power inherent in love
elegy has deserted him, a condition which is emphasized by the
Propertian imitation. Both of these elegies about failure contribute
to the pessimistic tone which permeates *Am.* 3.6-3.14.

Am. 3.9, the central poem of the third book, is a long lament over
the death of Tibullus. While the form is a traditional one, the
symbolic import of this elegy is tremendous.[15] The poem links elegy
and death in a very extensive and obvious way, and in so doing
continues the gloomy tone of Book Three. Yet *Am.* 3.9 is not all
depressing. Within this elegy Ovid sets forth his faith in the immortality of the written word, the triumph of poetry over death.
Thus near the mid-point of the poem he states:

Am. 3.9.39:
carminibus confide bonis: iacet ecce Tibullus.

It is important to note that even though *Am.* 3.9 was written to
honor Tibullus, Ovid does not speak strictly of love elegy. Rather,
poetry of any kind can triumph over death. This catholic view in a
poem about a dead love elegist is one more hint of Ovid's intentions.
Love elegy will not occupy him forever.

Am. 3.9 is 68 lines in length. It can be divided into four sections
of roughly sixteen lines each. In lines 1-16 Ovid discusses the reactions of Elegy, Venus and Cupid to Tibullus' death. In lines 17-32
he talks of the power of poetry to confer immortality. The last two
sections are concerned more strictly with Tibullus, the unfairness
of his death and then his funeral and reception in the Underworld.[16]

It is in the second section (17-32) that Ovid has included imitations of Propertius. Again, his purpose was contrast. Ovid is
attempting to show that all poetry is worthwhile and in so doing,
uses imitation to remind the reader of the more parochial attitude
of Propertius to whom only elegy was acceptable.

---

[15] This form is the epicedion. See E. Thomas, "A Comparative Analysis
of Ovid *Amores* II.6 and III.9" *Latomus* 24 (1965) 599-609.
[16] These last two sections, as we might expect, contain many imitations of
Tibullus. See J. H. Taylor, "*Amores* III.9: A Farewell to Elegy" *Latomus*
29 (1970) 474-77.

Ovid begins the second section of *Am.* 3.9 with a statement about the power of death over the poet.

Am. 3.9.17-20:

at sacri vates et divum cura vocamur,
   sunt etiam qui nos numen habere putent.
scilicet omne sacrum mors inportuna profanat;
   omnibus obscuras inicit illa manus.

Vates here is used to mean all poets, irrespective of the genre in which they write.[17] Later (29-32) Ovid emphasizes that immortality comes from any type of poetry by choosing his examples from opposite ends of the poetic spectrum. He first mentions Homer, the *Iliad* and the *Odyssey*, then the love elegy of Tibullus.

Two imitations of Propertius follow the four lines which open this section.

Prop. 2.13A.5-8:

non ut Pieriae quercus mea verba sequantur,
   aut possim Ismaria ducere valle feras,
sed magis ut nostro stupefiat Cynthia versu:
   tunc ego sim Inachio notior arte Lino.

Am. 3.9.21-24:

quid pater Ismario, quid mater profuit Orpheo,
   carmine quid victas obstipuisse feras?
et Linon in silvis idem pater 'aelinon' altis
   dicitur invita concinuisse lyra.

Prop. 2.13A is a very good example of Propertius' single minded devotion to love elegy and shows his parochialism at its zenith. The elegy begins with a statement of Propertius' desire to work only in the elegiac genre. (Amor is ordering the poet.)

Prop. 2.13A.3-4:

hic me tam gracilis vetuit contemnere Musas,
   iussit et Ascraeum sic habitare nemus.

---

[17] See J. K. Newman (Chapter II, note 1) 103. I disagree with his view that Ovid here is defining *vates* as a poet who draws inspiration from Homer.

The poem ends with a reiteration of Propertius' primary goal—to have his poetry read and liked by his mistress (11-16). Ovid through an imitation which brings to mind Prop. 2.13A has introduced the picture of the totally devoted elegist, a poet who would not think of leaving the elegiac genre.[18]

This figure is demolished in the next Propertian imitation which follows immediately.[19]

Prop. 3.3.51-52:

talia Calliope, lymphisque a fonte petitis
  ora Philitea nostra rigavit aqua.

Am. 3.9.25-26:

adice Maeoniden, a quo ceu fonte perenni
  vatum Pieriis ora rigantur aquis.

Once again the Propertian distich concerns the poet's exclusive devotion to love elegy. In fact, this is the final couplet in the programmatic poem in which both Apollo and the Muses warn Propertius to continue writing love elegy and to avoid the more serious poetic genres.

Ovid has made some very important changes in his imitation of these Propertian lines. First, Ovid has altered Propertius' ...*Philitea...aqua* to...*Pieriis...aquis.* Philitas, as an Alexandrian elegist, was a suitable source of inspiration only for those writing elegy. Pierian is a more general term applicable to any kind of poetry. Secondly, Ovid designates Homer, an epic poet, as the source of inspiration for poets. By these changes Ovid is rejecting Propertius' parochialism. Propertius can contemplate only elegy as a suitable genre for himself. Ovid takes a more liberal attitude towards genres other than elegy. Again, he is subtly indicating that his sojourn with love elegy is almost finished. Since other types of poetry will soon command his attention, he is careful to state that all kinds of poetry will endure beyond the grave.[20]

---

[18] There may also be some connection between Ovid's theme of death and Prop. 2.13B, an elegy in which Propertius describes his own death. The state of the text, however, makes it difficult to say with certainty that 2.13A and 2.13B were originally part of the same poem. For conjectures, see Smyth (Chapter IV, note 14) 47-50.

[19] Neumann, 11, claims that this was not made consciously (*consulto*) by Ovid.

[20] Ovid does not dwell on this point. In the three sections of *Am.* 3.9

The implications of *Am.* 3.9 become reality in 3.10 and 3.13, poems which can hardly be considered traditional love elegies. *Am.* 3.10 is similar to 3.6 in form. It begins and ends with a connection to a conventional subject: Ovid is complaining that due to the rites of Ceres, he must sleep alone.[21] The main section of the poem, however, is a mythological narrative about the powers of Ceres and her love for Iasius. As in *Am.* 3.6 the theme of love is retained, but embedded in a tale from mythology. 3.10, however, unlike 3.6, contains no allusions to Propertius. Indeed, in the three elegies which can be considered previews of the *Fasti* because of their subject matter, Ovid is moving farther and farther away from the theme of love. In *Am.* 3.6, the mythological narrative centered around love and there were strong ties to be found with Prop. 4.7. Now, in *Am.* 3.10 less than half of the mythological narrative deals with love and there are no links to Propertian elegy.[22] In *Am.* 3.13, the last of these elegies, we find nothing about love at all, not even an attempt by Ovid to connect the poem to himself and his girl friend.[23] Rather, he devotes the entire elegy to the relating of the details of a religious ceremony. *Am.* 3.13, like 3.10, contains no Propertian imitations.

The Propertian imitations in *Am.* 3.11 and 3.11b have already been discussed in terms of their importance in the construction of the poetic pair.[24] This poetic pair also adds to the general tone of failure that we have been tracing in Book Three. Just as *Am.* 3.10 corresponds roughly to *Am.* 3.6, 3.11 and 3.11b correspond roughly to *Am.* 3.7. In 3.7 Ovid was physically impotent. In 3.11 and 3.11b, he presents himself as mentally impotent. He resolves at the beginning of 3.11 to be done with his love affair but then, at the beginning of 3.11b tells us that he is incapable of carrying out his decision.

Am. 3.11b.33-34:

Luctantur pectusque leve in contraria tendunt
   hac amor, hac odium; sed, puto, vincit amor.

---

which speak directly of Tibullus, he is concerned only with elegy and the particular fame and immortality it has brought his dead friend. The theme we have been discussing because of the subtle way it is introduced does not intrude on Ovid's primary purpose of eulogizing Tibullus.

[21] See Prop. 2.33; Tib. 1.3.26.

[22] The theme of Ceres teaching the ways of agriculture to mankind (*Am.* 3.10.9-14) is actually used by Ovid in the *Fasti* (4.395-402).

[23] Indeed, in *Am.* 3.13.1 Ovid mentions his wife.

[24] See Chapter V, pages 83-85.

While Ovid's major Propertian imitation—the image of the garlanded ship reaching port (Prop. 3.24.15-18)—helps to prepare the reader for this shift in mood, there are other implications here. Prop. 3.24 and 3.25 mark the end of Propertius' love affair with Cynthia. By reminding us of the end of Propertius' third book, Ovid may indeed be hinting again at the impending end of his own three books of love elegy.

Evidence for this becomes stronger if we acknowledge the multiple thematic similarities between *Am.* 3.11, 3.11b and Prop. 3.24, 3.25.[25] For example, both Ovid and Propertius mention their contribution to the mistress' fame.

Prop. 3.24.3-4:

noster amor talis tribuit tibi, Cynthia, laudes:
  versibus insignem te pudet esse meis.

Am. 3.11.19-20:

scilicet et populo per me comitata placebas:
  causa fuit multis noster amoris amor.

Other themes common to both elegies include exclusion (Prop. 3.25.15, *Am.* 3.11.9), long suffering servitude (Prop. 3.25.3-4, *Am.* 3.11.1) and the trust of the girl in her beauty (Prop. 3.24.1, *Am.* 3.11b.41-44). Similarity of theme, of course, does not constitute proof of imitation. However, in *Am.* 3.11, 3.11b the number of themes similar to those of Prop. 3.24, 3.25, coupled with the true imitation of Prop. 3.24.14-18, clearly shows Ovid's desire for association with the last two poems of Propertius' love elegy. In the course of *Am.* 3.11, 3.11b, then, even though Ovid does not carry out his resolve to end his affair, we are given good reason to believe that the end is rapidly approaching. The emotional difficulties that Ovid claims prevented him from escaping from love will eventually be overcome. Just as Propertius broke with Cynthia in 3.24, 3.25, so shall Ovid achieve freedom, or at least that is what he implies through his imitations.

In *Am.* 3.12 Ovid reexamines the theme of the usefulness of love elegy to the lover-poet. In this it corresponds to *Am.* 3.8, where Ovid lamented the fact that his poetic talent no longer guaranteed

---

[25] These are listed by Neumann, 75-77.

him preference over his rivals. In 3.12 the poet comes to the conclusion that he never should have celebrated Corinna at all because his verse has made her famous and desirable to all men.

Am. 3.12.11-12:

me lenone placet, duce me perductus amator,
  ianua per nostras est adaperta manus.

As in 3.8, Ovid is admitting the failure of his love elegy. Poetry was supposed to win him his girl. In 3.8, we saw simple failure: talent no longer counted for anything. In *Am.* 3.12, however, talent is not simply neutral. Rather, Ovid's talent has become a source of harm in his suit for Corinna.[26] This negative tone is consistent with what we have already seen in Ovid's third book. As the end of the *Amores* approaches, Ovid is more anxious than ever to communicate his desire to progress to other poetic tasks. An elegy such as 3.12 insinuates that continuing to write love elegy will be totally counterproductive from the poet-lover's point of view.

In keeping with the pessimistic tone of *Am.* 3.12, Ovid in his first distich includes a Propertian imitation which carries overtones of gloom and even possible death.[27]

Prop. 2.28B.37-40:

et iam Luna negat totiens descendere caelo,
  nigraque funestum concinit omen avis.
una ratis fati nostros portabit amores
  caerula ad infernos velificata lacus.

Am. 3.12.1-2:

Quis fuit ille dies, quo tristia semper amanti
  omina non albae concinuistis aves?

The Propertian lines are from an elegy where Cynthia is lying sick and near death. Ovid's use of these particular lines at the beginning of *Am.* 3.12 serves to cast the shadow of death over the entire elegy. This is similar to the way Ovid linked the Anio River to the figure

---

[26] This is emphasized through the imitation of Prop. 2.8.5-6, discussed in Chapter IV, pages 48-50.

[27] The consensus of the Propertian manuscripts was *condidit*, not *concinit*. This was corrected by V₂, and *concinit* is generally accepted. See Smyth (Chapter IV, note 14) 70.

of the dead Cynthia in *Am.* 3.6, and indeed is in keeping with the general theme of death that is prevalent in the third book.[28]

Imitation of Propertius continues throughout the opening lines of the poem. Two more imitations are introduced in quick succession.

Prop. 2.8.5-6:

possum ego in alterius positam spectare lacerto?
  nec mea dicetur, quae modo dicta mea est?

Am. 3.12.5-6:

quae modo dicta mea est, quam coepi solus amare,
  cum multis vereor ne sit habenda mihi.

Prop. 2.25.3-4:

ista meis fiet notissima forma libellis,
  Calve, tua venia, pace, Catulle, tua.

Am. 3.12.7-8:

fallimur, an nostris innotuit illa libellis?
  sic erit: ingenio prostitit illa meo.

Both of these imitations help to emphasize Ovid's main point, the bankruptcy of the elegiac genre as a means of winning love. The first imitation accomplishes this through establishing Prop. 2.8 as a background poem. The contrast in attitude thus achieved is significant.[29]

Ovid's imitation of Prop. 2.25.3 serves to emphasize the traditional quality of the elegist's praise of his girl friend.[30] Not only does Propertius state that Cynthia will become famous, he mentions Calvus and Catullus, other poets who conferred fame on their girl friends. What Ovid has done, then, is an integral part of the elegiac

---

[28] This imitation also creates an anticlimax. We soon discover that Corinna is not dying, or even sick. The problem being discussed, in fact, is critical only from the poet's standpoint.

[29] See the earlier discussion of this imitation (*supra*, note 26).

[30] The word *libellis* greatly strengthens the case for imitation here. Augustan poets rarely used the word in regard to fame to be conferred by their poetry, perhaps because *libellus* is a diminutive. (For a discussion of the connotations of diminutives, see Axelson [Chapter III, note 30] 38 ff.) Other examples are *Am.* 2.17.33 and Prop. 3.2.17, a line which Newman [Chapter II, note 2] 395 claims is the basis for *Am.* 3.12.7. These lines, however, are in no way similar except for the word *libellis*.

tradition. At the end of his distich, however, Ovid invalidates the tradition in one quick stroke, ...*ingenio prostitit illa meo*. Writing poetry about a girl's beauty has developed into something sordid and crass. The crassness which now pervades this aspect of the elegiac tradition is emphasized twice more in the next several lines. Ovid calls his poetry *praeconia* (9) and himself *leno* (11).

That Ovid's purpose here was to demonstrate the uselessness of love elegy becomes apparent again a few lines later.

Am. 3.12.15-18:

cum Thebae, cum Troia foret, cum Caesaris acta,
    ingenium movit sola Corinna meum.
aversis utinam tetigissem carmina Musis,
    Phoebus et inceptum destituisset opus.

Although there is no evidence of direct Propertian imitation here, these lines (15-16) reflect common elegiac themes. The poet's dependence on his girl friend for his poetic material is usually stated with a proud flourish. We know that he prefers it that way.[31] In *Am.* 3.12 Ovid reverses this idea. He would have preferred to write epic. The love elegy inspired by Corinna should never have come into existence.[32]

The second half of *Am.* 3.12 (19-44) has as its subject the poet's power to make fiction credible. Although Ovid is disparaging this power, he still acknowledges that it exists (19-20, 43-44). Truth may be lacking but the poet with his power over words can make a myth or fable seem real. This theme leads directly into *Am.* 3.14, Ovid's farewell elegy to Corinna. Unlike Prop. 3.25, *Am.* 3.14 is not an elegy which is angry and hostile in tone. Rather, Ovid's attitude is one of resignation, a resignation so total and deep-seated that in a final act of desperation the poet transfers the power over the

---

[31] See. *e.g.*, *Am.* 2.17.34; Prop. 2.1.4; 2.30.40.
[32] The juxtaposition of the Muses and Apollo is reminiscent of Prop. 3.3, the programmatic elegy in which Propertius is given instructions on using his poetry to perpetuate the elegiac ideal of romance (47-50). It is interesting that Calliope tells Propertius:

nil tibi sit rauco praeconia classica cornu
    flare, nec Aonium tingere Marte nemus.
                                    (3.3.41-42)
Ovid has recently (line 9) referred to his love elegy as *praeconia*. This is his only use of the word in the *Amores*.

creation of illusion from himself to his girl friend. He begs Corinna to lie to him about her trysts and to deny the existence of her other lovers. He will give credence to her.

Am. 3.14.45-46:

> quae bene visa mihi fuerint, bene visa negato:
>   concedent verbis lumina nostra tuis.

In *Am.* 3.12 the creation of a believable fiction had negative results for Ovid, but at least he was the creator. In 3.14 the situation has completely changed as the following comparison shows.

Am. 3.12.43-44:

> et mea debuerat falso laudata videri
>   femina; credulitas nunc mihi vestra nocet.

Am. 3.14.29-30:

> da populo, da verba mihi: sine nescius errem
>   et liceat stulta credulitate frui.

For a poet to surrender the power of creating *credulitas* and to become credulous himself means the end of his poetry, Corinna has forced Ovid into this position and thus we are about to have the end of the *Amores*.

Ovid's total resignation and passivity becomes even more apparent when *Am.* 3.14 is read against the background of Prop. 2.32. Ovid has echoed Propertius at the beginning and end of *Am.* 3.14.[33]

Prop. 2.32.1-2:

> Qui videt, is peccat: qui te non viderit ergo,
>   non cupiet: facti lumina crimen habent.

Prop. 2.32.21-26:

> sed de me minus est: famae iactura pudicae
>   tanta tibi miserae, quanta meretur, erit.
> nuper enim de te nostras me laedit ad auris
>   rumor, et in tota non bonus urbe fuit.
> sed tu non debes inimicae credere linguae:
>   semper formosis fabula poena fuit.

---

[33] Neumann, 50-54, discusses the dependence of *Am.* 3.14 on Prop. 2.32. His conclusions, however, are vague: "Ovidius sententias a Propertio allatas variat vel in contrarias vertit." (52).

Am. 3.14.1-6:

Non ego, ne pecces, cum sis formosa, recuso,
    sed ne sit misero scire necesse mihi;
nec te nostra iubet fieri censura pudicam
    sed tamen ut temptes dissimulare rogat.
non peccat, quaecumque potest peccasse negare,
    solaque famosam culpa professa facit.

Immediately apparent here is Propertius' attitude of hopefulness
even in the face of damning evidence (3-20). The older elegist is
eager to excuse Cynthia for her misdeeds. He thus places the fault
on the men who see Cynthia (1-2), not on Cynthia herself. In lines
21-26 he totally discounts the rumors he has heard since evil rumor
always follows beautiful women. At the end of the elegy Propertius
seeks to excuse Cynthia's conduct on the basis of the customs of
the times (43-60).

The Ovidian attitude in *Am.* 3.14 is exactly the opposite. Ovid
presents himself as a lover who has completely lost hope and is
resigned to the faithlessness of his girl. This is emphasized in the
opening line of his elegy when the Propertian *is peccat* becomes *ne
pecces*. The girl friend, not the male suitor, deserves the blame.
Ovid also directly contradicts Propertius' statement about rumor
(25-26). Propertius urges Cynthia to ignore such things. Ovid urges
Corinna to create rumor, to lie in order to deceive him (4-6). The
difference in attitude is summed up in Ovid's change of the Propertian *tibi miserae* (22) to *misero mihi* (2). In each case, the innocent
party is *miser*. Propertius in giving this epithet to Cynthia is
furthering his efforts to believe her innocent. As the eternally hopeful lover, he has cast her in the role of victim. Ovid, however,
applies the word to himself. He knows Corinna is at fault. He is her
victim and a totally resigned one at that.

Ovid returns to the theme of Corinna's power to create illusion
at the end of *Am.* 3.14. Indeed, he almost begs her to exercise her
power: *...et falli muneris instar erit* (42). Ovid's hopelessness and
despair is heightened if we compare the end of *Am.* 3.14 with the
end of Prop. 2.32.

Am. 3.14.47-50:

prona tibi vinci cupientem vincere palma est,
    sit modo 'non feci' dicere lingua memor:
cum tibi contingat verbis superare duobus,
    etsi non causa, iudice vince tuo.

Prop. 2.32.59-62:

nec minus aerato Danae circumdata muro
    non potuit magno casta negare Iovi.
quod si tu Graias es tuque imitata Latinas,
    semper vive meo libera iudicio.

By the end of 2.32 Propertius has reached the point of accepting
Cynthia on her own terms. Ovid, however, is unable to do this. Only
if Corinna will create illusion for him, will make fiction seem like
reality through lying words, will he be able to continue the relationship. We are immediately struck by the total bankruptcy of the
relationship itself. Even more important is the fact that words in
this relationship will no longer have any concrete meaning. As
vehicles for any sort of effective communication, words have been
rendered useless by Ovid's pleas in this poem. Since Ovid, the poet-
lover is a man of words, the message is clear. The end of the *Amores*
is at hand.

Am. 3.6 through 3.14, then, form a collection of poems within a
collection of poems. They have much in common. First this group
of poems contains several elegies which preview other Ovidian
works, particularly the *Fasti* (3.6, 3.10, 3.13). Ovid is trying his hand
at *grandius opus* (3.1.70) even before he has closed his collection of
love elegy. Two of these "preview" poems contain no Propertian
imitations. *Am.* 3.6 contains imitation from Propertius' fourth
book (4.7).

Secondly, the themes of death, impotence and failure are prevalent in *Am.* 3.6-3.14. In almost every elegy Propertian imitation
is used by Ovid to emphasize these themes, generally through
contrast. Ovid is presenting himself as unable to continue writing
love elegy even if he wanted to. Both his sexual abilities and his
poetry have become ineffectual and impotent in the game of love.
Indeed, we see Ovid trace his verbal impotence from 3.8 (where his
poetry no longer gives him preference with his girl) to 3.12 (where
his poetry praising Corinna has been harmful to his suit by bringing
her other lovers) to 3.14 (where Ovid abandons altogether the idea
of "the power of words"). By reminding us through imitation of
Propertius' literary and sexual successes, Ovid underlines his own
despair.

Ovid, however, makes it clear that all of this is merely posturing.
Thus he concludes the entire collection with an elegy (3.15) which

expresses his faith in what he has created.[34] He refers to the *Amores* as *post mea mansurum fata superstes opus* (20). Similarly, in the midst of the elegy on the death of Tibullus (3.9) Ovid reaffirms his faith in the power of poetry to live on after death and render the poet immortal (17-32). His presentation of himself as a poetic failure can be viewed as a condescension to the conventions of the genre. Any collection of elegies ends with the poet-lover unhappy and miserable over the termination of his affair. Since the *Amores* is concerned just as much (if not more) with the literary form of elegy as with Corinna, it is not surprising that the end of the collection concentrates on both the failure of elegy and the failure of the relationship.[35] Both Ovid the elegist and Ovid the lover are thus rendered unhappy. It is a great relief, then, to reach *Am.* 3.15 where Ovid confirms what we suspected all along. The *Amores* are not a failure. Ovid may have "lost" Corinna, but in so doing has created a work which in his eyes rivals Vergil and Catullus.

---

[34] For a discussion of *Am.* 3.15, see Chapter II, pages 24-26.

[35] As G. Williams points out (Chapter I, note 17) 515, we need only compare the first and last poems of the *Amores* with those of Propertius' first three books to see how conscious of his literary form Ovid really was. He begins and ends with poetry. Propertius begins and ends with Cynthia. Williams goes even further: "It is symptomatic of the fact that Ovid is far more self-consciously literary in all his writing."

CHAPTER SEVEN

CONCLUSION

The artistry which is always present in Ovid's use of Propertian imitation has been amply demonstrated in the preceding chapters. Whether Ovid was writing a poetic pair, a programmatic poem, or a humorous narrative description, Propertian imitation could be used to enhance the meaning and effect of his elegy. The work of his predecessor was a valuable resource for the young Ovid, a resource to be judiciously and carefully employed. The individual poems of the *Amores* testify to the care which Ovid took in selecting Propertian passages for imitation and the skill with which he incorporated these imitations into his own work.

The specific effects for which Ovid was working have also been shown above. Ovid has imitated Propertius in order to create parody (Chapter III), or to achieve a surprise effect (Chapter V), or to emphasize that the end of his love elegy is at hand (Chapter VI). If we add to this Ovid's use of imitation to clarify differences in attitude between himself and Propertius (Chapters II and IV) or to create unity between the two parts of a poetic pair (Chapter V), Ovid's reasons for imitating his predecessor are indeed varied.

Yet for all of its variety, every Propertian imitation in the *Amores* is included for a reason. The needs of Ovid's own elegy dictated the selection of lines to be imitated. That Ovid did indeed view Prop. I-III as a resource to be used at his discretion is indicated by the random distribution of the imitations used in the *Amores*.[1] Except for the programmatic poems, where Ovid does limit his imitations to Propertian programmatic poems, there is not necessarily a correlation of subject matter. So in *Am.* 1.6, Ovid's paraclausithyron, none of the imitations are from Prop. 1.16. Yet both Ovid's *lena* poem (*Am.* 1.8) and his propempticon (*Am.* 2.11) do contain imitations from the Propertian elegies on these subjects (4.5, 1.8).[2]

---

[1] There are nine imitations from Propertius' first book, twenty-two from his second, thirteen from his third, a random distribution if one considers the varying lengths of the three books. In calculating these figures, a Propertian poem imitated several times within the same Ovidian elegy (such as Prop. 2.25 in *Am.* 2.4) has been counted as a single imitation.

[2] Ovid did, however, have his "favorite" Propertian poems. Prop. 2.22A, 2.25 and 3.3 are each used by him in four different elegies of the *Amores*.

The random selection of Propertian poems for imitation does not continue into Book IV.[3] Ovid makes great use of Prop. 4.1 in his programmatic poems (*Am.* 1.15, 3.1, 3.15). Aside from this, though, he limits his imitation of Book IV to the less serious elegies of the book, namely the two Cynthia elegies (4.7, 4.8) and the *lena* poem (4.5). Ovid's different method of selection in regard to Prop. IV seems to demand an explanation. Unfortunately, the evidence about dating is too scanty to permit more than a suggestion.[4] One possible explanation is that *Am.* 1.15, 3.1, 3.15, 1.8, 1.6 and 3.6, the elegies in which Ovid imitated from Prop. IV, were all written late, for the second edition of the *Amores* or at least near the end of Ovid's work on the first edition. Or might we suppose that Prop. 4.5, 4.7 and 4.8 were available to Ovid before the rest of Prop. IV?[5] The possibilities are intriguing but ultimately unprovable.

More can be said about Ovid's general method of imitation. No matter what effect he is trying to achieve or what section of Propertius he is imitating Ovid's basic technique is the same. The imitation is expected to recall context. Ovid is neither evoking a general Propertian "flavor" by his imitation, nor is he offering vague "compliments" to his predecessor. Rather, he expects his reader to identify the specific Propertian elegy being imitated. To appreciate fully the nuances of the imitation, the reader must thoroughly know the elegy, or at least that section of the elegy which precedes and follows the lines imitated. Ovid assumed that his readers possessed a knowledge of Propertius, a knowledge of enough depth that an imitation would bring to mind a specific Propertian context.

Once the context has been established, Ovid proceeds in one of two ways. More commonly he contrasts his context with the Propertian one. A variety of the effects discussed in the preceding chapters depend upon this device. For example, removing lines from a serious context and placing them in a lighter one creates parody.[6] An ironic effect is gained by introducing a Propertian

---

[3] Book IV, which is roughly the same length as Book III, provides Ovid with only six imitations.

[4] On dating the *Amores* and the fourth book of Propertius, see Chapter I, pages 5-6.

[5] G. Luck, "Das Acanthisgedicht des Properz" *Hermes* 83 (1955) 428-38 argues for a date of 28-27 B.C. for Prop. 4.5.

[6] See Chapter III.

context which is wholly at odds with the statement Ovid is ostensibly making in his poem.[7] Ovid also uses contrast of context to make serious statements about his view of poetry as compared to Propertius'.[8] Other attitudes, either serious or light, can also be compared and commented upon. Thus when Ovid's *lena* begins her speech with an imitation of the first line of Prop. 2.22A (*Am.* 1.8.23), the comparison of the contexts is very important.[9] Ovid has an old woman giving "immoral" advice to a girl. Propertius has the poet-lover saying the same thing about himself and in no way thinking it immoral. The contrasting situations make the point for Ovid. "Immorality" is a relative thing.

Secondly and less often, Ovid establishes similarity of context. This technique is useful when Ovid wants to emphasize the traditional aspect of his poetry. So in *Am.* 3.1.1-6, he describes a setting which imitates that of Prop. 3.3.25-28.[10] Ovid's extensive use of Prop. 4.5 in *Am.* 1.8 makes us aware of the traditional place of the *lena* figure in elegy. In this case, however, the "appeal to tradition" accentuates the untraditional aspects of Ovid's *lena*.[11] Imitation which establishes similarity of context is also used for an occasional special effect. The "hints" provided at the end of the first poem of a poetic pair are imitations of this sort.[12] The Propertian context in its broader sense will become Ovid's context at the beginning of the second poem of the pair. Surprise is also based on this technique. Similarity of context is established, then deliberately destroyed.[13]

All of the Propertian imitations in the *Amores*, then, ultimately depend upon recall of context for their success. Yet by establishing this, we have established only the broadest of common denominators. It is the genius of Ovid imposed upon the raw material of imitation which makes Propertian imitation in the *Amores* important. In Ovid's hands imitation becomes a means for adding something—a

---

[7] See, for example, the discussion of *Am.* 1.3 in Chapter IV; *Am.* 2.11 in Chapter V.

[8] See Chapter II; also the discussion of *Am.* 3.9 in Chapter VI.

[9] This is discussed at length in Chapter IV, pages 66-67. Other examples of imitation which result in comparison of attitude are also given in Chapter IV.

[10] See Chapter II, pages 17-18.

[11] See Chapter IV, pages 59-68.

[12] The poetic pairs are discussed in the second half of Chapter V. The use of "hints" applies to *Am.* 2.13, 14; 2.9, 9b; 3.11, 11b.

[13] See the first half of Chapter V.

nuance or hidden meaning—to a particular elegy. The subtle artistry of the imitations discussed in this study should dispel the picture of the young Ovid as a poetaster who had memorized bits of earlier elegy. The imitations of Propertius in the *Amores* are carefully thought out, artistic additions to Ovid's own poems. And so from a study of Ovid, the Propertian imitator, we have discovered much about Ovid, the creative artist.

BIBLIOGRAPHY

TEXTS AND COMMENTARIES

Barber, E.A., *Sexti Properti Carmina.*[2] Oxford, 1960.
Barsby, J. A., *Ovid: Amores Book I.* Oxford, 1973.
Brandt, P., *P. Ovidi Nasonis Amorum Libri Tres.* Leipzig, 1911; repr. Hildesheim, 1963.
Butler, H. E., *Sexti Properti Opera Omnia.* London, 1905.
Butler, H. E. and Barber, E. A., *The Elegies of Propertius.* Oxford, 1933.
Camps, W. A., *Propertius: Elegies, Books I, II, III, IV.* Cambridge, 1961, 1967, 1966, 1965.
Enk, P. J., *Sex. Properti Elegiarum Liber I (Monobiblos), II* (2 vols.). Leiden, 1946, 1962.
Kenney, E. J., *P. Ovidi Nasonis Amores, Medicamina Faciei Femineae, Ars Amatoria, Remedia Amoris.* Oxford, 1961.
Munari, F., *P. Ovidi Nasonis Amores.*[5] Firenze, 1970.
Rothstein, M., *Die Elegien des Sextus Propertius.*[2] 1st and 2nd parts. Berlin, 1920, 1924.
Schuster, M. and Dornseiff, F., *Sex. Properti Elegiarum Libri IV.*[2] Leipzig, 1958.

OTHER WORKS

Allen, A. W., "Sincerity and the Roman Elegists," *CP* 45 (1950) 145-60.
Axelson, B., *Unpoetische Wörter.* Lund, 1945.
Barsby, J. A., "*Desultor Amoris* in *Amores* 1.3," *CP* 70 (1975) 44-45.
——, "The Composition and Publication of the First Three Books of Propertius," *G &R* 21 (1974) 128-37.
Berman, K., "A Note on Propertius 2.16.41-42," *CP* 66 (1971) 110-12.
Bömer, F., "Ovid und die Sprache Vergils," *Gymnasium* 66 (1959) 268-88.
Boucher, J.-P., *Études sur Properce.* Paris, 1965.
Bréguet, E., "*In una parce duobus:* Thème et Clichés," *Hommages à L. Hermann, Collection Latomus* 44 (1960) 205-14.
Burck, E., "Römische Wesenszüge der augusteischen Liebeselegie," *Hermes* 80 (1952) 163-200.
Cameron, A., "The First Edition of Ovid's *Amores*," *CQ* 18 (1968) 320-33.
Cèbe, J., *La caricature et la parodie dans le monde romain antique des origines à Juvénal.* Paris, 1966.
Clausen, W., "Callimachus and Latin Poetry," *GRBS* 5 (1965) 181-96.
Copley, F. O., *Exclusus Amator, A Study in Latin Love Poetry. Phil. Monographs of the APA* 17 (1956).
——, "*Servitium Amoris* in the Roman Elegists," *TAPA* 78 (1947) 285-300.
Cordier, A., *Études sur le vocabulaire épique dans l'Énéide.* Paris, 1939.
Curran, L. C., "*Desultores amoris*: Ovid *Amores* 1.3," *CP* 61 (1966) 47-49.
——, "Ovid, *Amores* 1.10," *Phoenix* 18 (1964) 314-18.
Day, A., *The Origins of Latin Love Elegy.* Oxford, 1938.
Dickson, T. W., "Borrowed Themes in Ovid's *Amores*," *CJ* 59 (1964) 175-80.
Donnet, D., "Ovide, Properce et l'élégie latine," *LEC* 33 (1965) 253-79.
Du Quesnay, I.M. Le M., "The *Amores*" in *Ovid*, Binns, J. W., editor. London, 1973. 1-48.

Elliott, A. G., "*Amores* 1.13: Ovid's Art," *CJ* 69 (1973-4) 127-32.
Ferguson, J., "Catullus and Ovid," *AJP* 81 (1960) 337-57.
Fränkel, H., *Ovid, A Poet between Two Worlds*. Berkeley, 1945.
Frécaut, J., *L'esprit et l'humour chez Ovide*. Grenoble, 1972.
Ganzenmüller, C., "Aus Ovids Werkstatt," *Philol.* 70 (1911) 274-311.
Goold, G. P., "Amatoria Critica," *HSCP* 69 (1965) 1-107.
——, "Noctes Propertianae," *HSCP* 71 (1966) 59-106.
Görler, W., "Ovids Propemptikon (*Amores* 2.11)," *Hermes* 93 (1965) 338-47.
Gross, N., "Ovid, *Amores* 3.11 A and B: A Literary Mélange," *CJ* 71 (1975-6) 152-60.
Guillemin, A., "L'imitation dans les litteratures antiques et en particulière dans la litterature latine," *REL* 2 (1924) 35-57.
Heinze, R., "Ovids elegische Erzählung," *S. Akad. Lpz., phil.-hist. Kl.*, Band 71, Heft 7 (1919). Repr. in *Vom Geist des Römertums*, Leipzig, 1960, 308-402.
Housman, A. E., "Emendationes Propertianae," *JP* 16 (1888) 1-35.
Hubbard, M., *Propertius*. London, 1974.
Jacoby F., "Zur Entstehung der römischen Elegie," *RhM* 60 (1905) 38-105.
Jäger, F., *Das antike Propemptikon und das 17 Gedicht des Paulinus von Nola*. Diss. München, 1913.
Jäger, K., *Zweigliedrige Gedichte und Gedichtpaare bei Properz und in Ovids Amores*. Diss. Tübingen, 1967.
Kenney, E. J., "Nequitiae Poeta," *Ovidiana Recherches sur Ovide*. Paris, 1958. 201-9.
——, "On the *Somnium* Attributed to Ovid," *Agon* 3 (1969) 1-14.
Knoche, U., "Gedanken und Vorschläge zur Interpretation von Properzens Gedicht II.28," in *Miscellanea Properziana. Atti dell' Accad. Properziana del Subasio* V.5 (1957). Repr. in *Antike Lyrik*, Eisenhut, W., ed. Darmstadt, 1970. 379-401.
——, "Zur Frage der Properzinterpolation," *RhM* 85 (1936) 8-63.
Kornzeniewski, D., "Ovids elegisches Proömium," *Hermes* 92 (1964) 182-213.
Kratins, O., "The Pretended Witch: A Reading of Ovid's *Am.* 1.8," *PhQ* 42 (1963) 151-58.
Kühn, W., "Die Meerfahrt der Corinna. Ovid, *Am.* 2.11," *Festschrift Karl Büchner*. Wiesbaden, 1970. 151-59.
Lee, A. G., "Tenerorum Lusor Amorum," in *Critical Essays on Roman Literature, Elegy and Lyric*, Sullivan, J. P., ed. Cambridge, Mass., 1962.
Lefèvre, E., *Propertius ludibundus*. Heidelberg, 1966.
Lelièvre, F. J., "The Basis of Ancient Parody," *G&R*, 2nd ser. 1 (1954) 66-81.
Lenz, F. W., "Junofest (Ovid *Amores* III.13)," *Fabula* 1 (1957-58) 255-62.
Löfstedt, E., "Reminiscence and Imitation. Some Problems in Latin Literature," *Eranos* 47 (1949) 148-64.
Luck, G., "Das Acanthisgedicht des Properz," *Hermes* 83 (1955) 428-38.
——, "Der Dichter zwischen Elegie und Epos," in *Antike Lyrik*, Eisenhut, W., ed. Darmstadt, 1970. 464-79.
——, *The Latin Love Elegy*. New York, 1960.
MacKay, L. A., "Umbrian Rimbaud," *G&R* 17 (1970) 177-83.
Martini, E., *Einleitung zu Ovid. Schrif. der Philos. Fak. der Dt. Univ. in Prag.* 12 (1933).
McGann, M. M. J., "The Date of Tibullus' Death," *Latomus* 29 (1970) 774-80.
Müller, L., "De Ovidi Amorum libris," *Philol.* 11 (1856) 60-91.
Murgatroyd, P., "*Militia Amoris* and the Roman Elegists," *Latomus* 34 (1975) 59-79.

Nethercut, W. R., "The Ironic Priest: Propertius' Roman Elegies III.1-5: Imitations of Horace and Vergil," *AJP* 91 (1970) 385-407.

Neumann, R., *Qua ratione Ovidius in Amoribus scribendis Properti elegiis usus sit.* Diss. Göttingen, 1919.

Newman, J. K., *Augustus and the New Poetry. Collection Latomus* 88 (1967).

——, *The Concept of Vates in Augustan Poetry. Collection Latomus* 89 (1967).

Norden, E., *Vergilius Aeneis VI.*⁴ Stuttgart, 1957.

Oliver, R. P., "The First Edition of the *Amores,*" *TAPA* 76 (1945) 191-215.

Olstein, K., "*Amores* 1.3 and Duplicity as a Way of Love," *TAPA* 105 (1975) 241-57.

Otis, B., "Ovid and the Augustans," *TAPA* 69 (1938) 188-229.

——, *Ovid as an Epic Poet.*² Cambridge, 1970.

Platnauer, M., *Latin Elegiac Verse.* Cambridge, 1951.

Puelma, M., "Die Vorbilder der Elegiendichtung in Alexandrien und Rom," *MusHel* 11 (1954) 101-16.

Quinn, K., *Latin Explorations.* London, 1963.

Reitzenstein, E., "Das neue Kunstwollen in den Amores Ovids," *RhM* 84 (1935) 62-88.

——, *Wirklichkeitsbild und Gefühlsentwicklung bei Properz. Philol. Suppl.* 29, Heft 2. (1936).

Richmond, J. A., "On Imitation in Ovid's 'Ibis' and in the 'Halieutica' Ascribed to Him," in *Atti del Convegno Internazionale Ovidiano,* Vol. II. Rome, 1959. 9-57.

Ross, D. O., Jr., *Backgrounds to Augustan Poetry: Gallus, Elegy and Rome.* Cambridge, 1975.

Shackleton Bailey, D. R., *Propertiana.* Cambridge, 1956.

Smyth, W. R., *Thesaurus Criticus ad Sexti Properti Textum. Mnem.* suppl. 12 (1970).

Stoessl, F., "Ovids Lebensentscheidung," in *Festschrift K. Vretska.* Heidelberg, 1970. 250-75.

Sullivan, J. P., "Two Problems in Roman Love Elegy," *TAPA* 92 (1961) 522-36.

Taylor, J. H., "*Amores* III.9: A Farewell to Elegy," *Latomus* 29 (1970) 474-77.

Thomas, E., "A Comparative Analysis of Ovid *Amores* II.6 and III.9," *Latomus* 24 (1965) 599-609.

——, "Ovid at the Races. *Amores* III.2; *Ars amatoria* I.135-164," in *Hommages à M. Renard.* Brussels, 1969. 710-24.

——, "Variations on a Military Theme in Ovid's *Amores,*" *G&R* 11 (1964) 151-65.

Tränkle, H., *Die Sprachkunst des Properz und die Tradition der lateinischen Dichtersprache. Hermes* Einzelschr. 15 (1960).

Wilkinson, L. R., "Greek Influence on the Poetry of Ovid," *Entretiens sur l'antiquité classique, Fondation Hardt* 2 (1956) 223-43.

——, *Ovid Recalled.* Cambridge, 1955.

Williams, G., *Tradition and Originality in Roman Poetry.* Oxford, 1968.

Wimmel, W., *Kallimachos in Rom. Hermes* Einzelschr. 16 (1960).

Winniczuk, L., "Cornelius Gallus und Ovid," *Dt. Akad. der Wissensch., Sektion für Altertumswissensch.* 22 (1960) 24-36.

Wlosok, A., "Die dritte Cynthia-Elegie des Properz," *Hermes* 95 (1967) 330-52. Repr. in *Antike Lyrik.* Eisenhut, W., ed. Darmstadt, 1970. 405-30.

Yardley, J. C., "Comic Influences in Propertius," *Phoenix* 26 (1972) 134-39.

Zingerle, A., *Ovidius und sein Verhältnis zu den Vorgängern und gleichzeitigen römischen Dichtern.* Innsbruck, 1869-71.

INDEX RERUM

INDEX LOCORUM PROPERTIANORUM ET OVIDIANORUM

PROPERTIUS

OVID

Amores

Ars

R.A.

Tristia

Printed in the United States
By Bookmasters